OPPORTUNITIES

Petroleum Careers

D0167423

OPPORTUNITIES in Petroleum Careers

REVISED EDITION

GRETCHEN KRUEGER

New York Chicago San Francisco Lisbon London Madrid Mexico City
Milan New Delhi San Juan Seoul Singapore Sydney Toronto

The McGraw·Hill Companies

Library of Congress Cataloging-in-Publication Data

Krueger, Gretchen Dewailly, 1952–
Opportunities in petroleum careers / by Gretchen Krueger.
p. cm.
Includes bibliographical references.
ISBN 0-07-149307-7 (alk. paper)
1. Petroleum industry and trade—Vocational guidance. I. Title.

HD9560.5.K782 2008
338.2′728023—dc22 2007047008

Copyright © 2008 by The McGraw-Hill Companies, Inc. All rights reserved. Printed in the United States of America. Except as permitted under the United States Copyright Act of 1976, no part of this publication may be reproduced or distributed in any form or by any means, or stored in a database or retrieval system, without the prior written permission of the publisher.

1 2 3 4 5 6 7 8 9 10 11 12 13 14 15 16 17 18 19 20 DOC/DOC 0 9 8

ISBN 978-0-07-149307-9
MHID 0-07-149307-7

Interior design by Rattray Design

McGraw-Hill books are available at special quantity discounts to use as premiums and sales promotions or for use in corporate training programs. To contact a representative, please visit the Contact Us pages at www.mhprofessional.com.

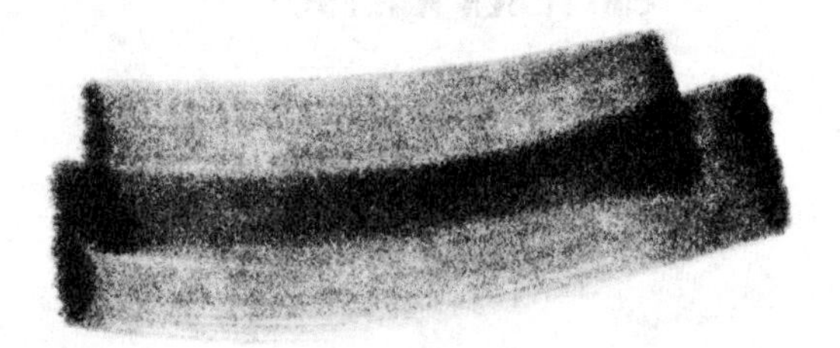

This book is printed on acid-free paper.

Contents

FOREWORD

THE PETROLEUM INDUSTRY is one of the most exciting industries to work in today. No other business in the world touches our lives in so many ways.

The American Petroleum Institute estimates that in just one twenty-four-hour period in the United States, the industry delivers energy to heat 80 million homes; supplies 382 million gallons of gasoline to service stations, enabling 200 million drivers to travel 8.5 billion road miles every day and to go about their daily routines; and transports 67 million gallons of gasoline to airport terminals, enabling 30,000 flights to travel 3.4 million air miles per day.

Almost six million people in the United States go to work each day in jobs that are either directly or indirectly tied to the petroleum industry.

Today, however, the energy industry is at a crossroads. Faced with an ever-increasing demand for oil and natural gas, we find ourselves without the necessary workforce to find, drill, refine, and transport the hundreds of products that make our lives more comfortable. The cyclical nature of the business, combined with an aging workforce, has taken its toll.

We are a mature industry, and the generations of workers who helped us reach the pinnacle of our success are ready to retire. But, before they go, they want to know that the workers who follow them will be properly trained and ready to take the helm.

In both the United States and Canada, the petroleum industry is focused on attracting the best and the brightest of this generation to continue the deep traditions of this industry, with a combination of hard work and excitement that creates opportunities for all.

Each year millions of dollars are spent to improve the technology used in the search for natural resources to protect the environment and to invest in our communities. These ongoing efforts will continue to provide opportunities for those seeking a career in the energy industry.

As we move farther from our shores and drill deeper into the earth, the commitment to husband our natural resources wisely remains. It will be up to you, the next generation of petroleum workers, to maintain a safe, secure, and sustainable energy future for generations to come.

Martha Wyrsch, President and CEO
Spectra Energy Transmission

Acknowledgments

I MARVEL AT the amount of information so readily available in our public libraries, at our universities, and, especially, on the multitude of Internet websites so easily found and navigated. A huge thank you goes to all the unknown individuals who develop and keep these websites updated.

This revision of *Opportunities in Petroleum Careers* includes a separate chapter on Canada, so much appreciation goes to my Canadian colleague Cathy Bennett, with Spectra Energy's Human Resources Department in Calgary, who pointed me in the right direction to update information on Canada.

Thanks also to Jaimè Croft Larsen, manager, marketing and communications, with the Petroleum Human Resources Council of Canada, who directed me to numerous Canadian websites that provided much detailed information for job seekers.

Grateful acknowledgment is made to Service Canada for permission to reprint salary and employment prospect information for Canadian jobs throughout this book. Information cited from Service Canada or Job Futures/Emploi-Avenir (jobfutures.ca, 2007) is reproduced with the permission of the Minister of Public Works and Government Services Canada, 2007.

I also want to acknowledge the American Petroleum Institute for its continuous leadership throughout the years in educating the public about the petroleum industry. The organization's websites are a great starting place for those who want to know more about this industry.

And a very special thanks goes to Martha Wyrsch, president and CEO of my company, Spectra Energy Transmission, who graciously agreed to pen the foreword for this book and who is a true believer in the future of this industry.

Introduction

As I RESEARCHED information for the second edition of *Opportunities in Petroleum Careers*, I realized that not much has changed in the petroleum industry from when the book was first released in 1990.

We are still at war in the Mideast. The Organization of Petroleum Exporting Countries (OPEC) has not regained its stature as the global powerhouse. Technology continues to bring us to new levels in our search for petroleum. And the industry continues to be faced with the lack of qualified and trained personnel.

As Spectra Energy Transmission president Martha Wyrsch notes in the Foreword, the energy industry is at a defining moment in its history. No longer can we count on multigenerational families to provide a steady stream of workers. Many workers have retired, and our younger generation appears to be interested in more trendy careers such as those in high-tech fields.

Juxtaposed against this scenario, as we move toward the end of the first decade of the twenty-first century, is an increasing demand for petroleum, despite the talk about conservation and alternative fuels.

Even with the growth in other energy sources such as biofuels, the Energy Information Administration's 2007 outlook predicts that oil, coal, and natural gas are expected to provide more than 80 percent of the United States' primary energy supply at least until 2030.

Added to this energy mix is the entry into the market of liquefied natural gas (LNG)—a source of energy that is expected to grow to fifty-five billion cubic feet a day by 2030. This source of energy will be transported by tanker from international markets, processed in the United States and Canada, and then transported to markets via pipeline.

To help meet projected growth in U.S. energy demands, oil and gas companies invested $98 billion from 2000 through 2005 on emerging energy technologies in the North American market.

As the demand for energy grows, job opportunities in the petroleum industry also should expand, particularly since there already is a growing need for personnel to replace the aging energy workforce. There are many careers and opportunities available with major energy companies, smaller independent companies, and with companies that provide services and equipment to the industry.

Opportunities in Petroleum Careers gives a detailed explanation of how petroleum is found, taken out of the ground, and made into the products we use every day. This book details a wide range of career opportunities in today's petroleum industry, as well as the outlook for employment into the next decade.

New to this revised edition is a chapter that addresses the outlook for petroleum employment in Canada. The glossary of energy terms has been updated to include current terms. Also included is a bibliography of sources and recommended reading, and appendixes listing where to go for more information, as well as colleges and universities specializing in petroleum careers. The appendix on organizations and associations has been greatly expanded and includes updated websites for easy access to information.

Opportunities in Petroleum Careers is an excellent source of information for anyone thinking about embarking on a career in the petroleum industry.

1

How We Use Petroleum Products Every Day

The petroleum extracted from the earth touches our lives in ways most of us can only imagine. This natural resource keeps our economic engine running, provides the foundation for products that make our lives easier, and allows us to live longer, quality lives.

In addition to fueling our cars, heating our homes, and cooking our foods, did you know that petroleum products are the basis for the heart valve replacements that may someday save our lives, the DVDs we watch our favorite movies on, and even the shampoos we use to wash our hair?

These petroleum products—primarily oil and natural gas—supply 65 percent of our nation's energy as well as help generate the electricity that powers our daily lives.

The United States is the third-largest oil producing country in the world, with more than five hundred thousand producing wells and approximately four thousand oil and natural gas platforms operating in U.S. waters. Canada is the world's third-largest producer of natural gas and seventh-largest producer of crude oil. Combined, the two countries produce about seven million barrels of crude oil a day.

The United States also is one of the largest consumers of petroleum products, though there is growing demand coming from emerging economies such as China and India. In the United States alone, about twenty million barrels are used each day—about three gallons per person—according to the American Petroleum Institute (API). The API is a national trade association that represents all aspects of America's oil and natural gas industry, and there is a wealth of information on its website at www.api.org and related sites at www.energytomorrow.org, www.adventuresinenergy.org, and www.classroom-energy.org.

Oil provides about 40 percent of the energy Americans consume and 97 percent of our transportation fuels. Natural gas provides 25 percent of our energy needs. Oil and natural gas are found all over the world in varying concentrations. The United States imports approximately 60 percent of its oil, with the majority coming from Canada and Mexico, while 84 percent of our natural gas is domestically produced.

The Energy Information Agency, the U.S. government's independent statistical and analytical agency within the U.S. Department of Energy (www.eia.doe.gov), projects that the demand for energy will grow at an average annual rate of 1.1 percent. Natural gas demand is expected to continue to increase to thirty trillion cubic feet (Tcf) by the year 2020.

With the demand for petroleum increasing, the good news is that there is an abundance of domestic oil and gas resources in the United States. The latest estimates reveal that there are more than 131 billion barrels of oil and more than a thousand Tcf of natural gas remaining to be discovered in the United States.

The amount here is enough oil to power 55 million cars for 30 years and heat 24 million homes for 30 years. And there is enough natural gas to heat 60 million homes that use natural gas for 120 years.

Petroleum: A Chemical "Black Gold"

So, what is petroleum and where does it come from? By definition, petroleum, in the strictest sense of the word, is crude oil as it comes out of the ground. It is a mixture of several chemical compounds, primarily hydrogen and carbon. In a broader sense, and for the purposes of this book, petroleum also is defined as all hydrocarbons, including oil, natural gas, natural gas liquids, and all related products. Petroleum also can exist as a solid, such as the tar sands found in some parts of Canada and the oil shale beds located in some western states.

Even after two hundred years, the origin of black gold, as it is sometimes called, remains the subject of debate. Since the mid-nineteenth century, scientists have variously believed that petroleum comes from coal, decayed animals and vegetables, and even volcanic matter. Today, the debate still continues in some scientific circles as to whether oil is organic (plant or vegetable matter) or inorganic (not living).

The general consensus among the majority of the earth's scientists, however, is that the petroleum produced today was formed over a period of millions of years when plant and animal matter was compressed as it settled at the bottom of prehistoric seabeds. This matter, covered with layers and layers of sediment, was changed into hydrocarbons through a combination of factors, including bacteria, heat, and pressure.

Oil was first believed to flow under the earth much like an underground stream of water. Further study throughout the years led scientists to learn that oil actually exists between geological structures in areas called *reservoirs*. The Society of Petroleum Engineers (SPE), one of the industry's largest professional organizations, compares a reservoir rock to a tray of marbles, with oil occupying the open spaces between the grains of rock.

Oil reservoirs may be a few thousand or many thousands of feet below the surface. How permeable—or how easily the oil or gas flows through connecting pore spaces—determines how easy it is to remove the petroleum from the ground. How petroleum is found and removed from these reservoirs will be discussed in Chapter 4.

Petroleum First Used to Light Fires

Scientists believe that the earliest use of petroleum occurred when natural seepages of both crude oil and natural gas were used by primitive tribes to light their fires. According to several versions of the story of the Great Flood, Noah used pitch—a form of natural asphaltic petroleum—as a caulking material to waterproof his ark.

Indian tribes are said to have used asphalt from the seeps at Santa Barbara, California, as a sealant for their canoes, as well as for war paints and medicines. And archaeologists believe the ancient Egyptians used the same substance as a lubricant on chariot wheels. The

Greeks are said to have used petroleum to set the sea on fire to destroy a fleet of ships belonging to an enemy that was threatening invasion.

It is thought that by the Middle Ages, Sicilians were gathering oil off their coast to use as fuel for lamps. Europeans, in the meantime, skimmed the natural springs for oil that they used for medicinal purposes, as well as for fuel.

It was the Chinese, however, who first drilled for petroleum. Using primitive drilling tools, they bored eight hundred feet into the earth in 347 A.D.—fifteen centuries before the birth of the modern-day petroleum industry!

Natural Gas

The Chinese also were the first to use natural gas—two thousand years ago—to evaporate seawater for salt. Like oil, natural gas was formed millions of years ago from organic matter compressed by mud and sand as it lay on the bottom of oceans. When the top layers hardened into rock, it created tremendous pressure and, combined with the heat from the earth, the organic matter became what we now call *fossil fuels*. Most natural gas is found in areas located near prehistoric mountain ranges.

Other early users were the North American colonists who found that natural gas seeping into creeks and swamps could be ignited. William A. Hart, who is commonly known as the father of natural gas, drilled the first commercial well in 1821 in Fredonia, New York. Hart, a gunsmith by trade, dug a twenty-seven-foot well near a natural gas spring and piped natural gas through hollow logs to nearby stores. In 1858 the Fredonia Gas Light Company was established to provide gas service to local residents.

When the blue flame gas burner was invented in 1855, it allowed gas to burn efficiently with a hot, smokeless flame. This paved the way for the use of gas for cooking purposes. By 1890, 500 miles of pipe carried natural gas to homes and businesses in Pittsburgh, Pennsylvania, making that city the first large-scale user of the fuel. By the 1950s, pipelines were in place across the country, transporting natural gas to distant markets.

Colonel Edwin L. Drake and His "Folly"

By the middle of the nineteenth century, Americans were using oil and gas taken directly from natural deposits on the earth's surface. While they knew these substances burned and could, therefore, be used for light, these pioneers still preferred to use whale oil and tallow candles for heating and lighting purposes. When whale oil began to become more scarce and, as a result, more expensive, Americans decided to search for an alternative fuel source. These early oil users soon found, however, that the three-gallon-per-day production they were getting from naturally occurring oil pools was not nearly enough to meet the growing demands of an expanding nation.

In 1854 Yale University Professor Benjamin Sillman and a group of businesspeople, headed by James M. Townsend, formed what is probably the first oil company in the world—the Pennsylvania Rock Oil Company. This company later became the Seneca Oil Company.

The group possessed a report that detailed the suitability of petroleum as a lighting fuel. Based on this report, the group members decided to attempt the recovery of large amounts of petroleum by taking a cue from water well diggers: they would drill for it.

These early oil people hired retired railroad conductor Colonel Edwin L. Drake to drill along the banks of Oil Creek at Titusville, Pennsylvania, an area located near an old oil spring. To drill the well, Drake's crew used an old steam engine with an iron bit connected to a rope. This was attached to a wooden winch mechanism they used for hoisting. After months of tedious drilling, the crew hit rock at the thirty-foot level. Boring through this hard surface was even more difficult, and the crew's progress slowed down to only three feet a day. By this time, the company's investors were growing more and more disgruntled at the lack of finding oil and named the operation "Drake's Folly."

On August 27, 1859, at sixty-nine and a half feet, a dark green liquid spewed a few feet in the air from the well. By the second day, the well was producing eight to ten barrels of oil a day, and Drake's drillers made history as the first to drill a well for the express purpose of finding oil.

History books, while covering the significance of the Pennsylvania discovery, rarely mention a second related historical event. On October 7, 1859, the well was destroyed when gas from the well ignited. New equipment was moved in shortly thereafter, and the well was revived. Thus, Drake's Folly also is recorded in petroleum history as the first oil-well fire on record. But more important, the Pennsylvania Rock Oil Company had proved the feasibility of boring through the earth's crust for a substance that was to change the world forever. The oil boom was on.

Spindletop Boom

Just like the gold rush to California only ten years earlier, oil towns sprang up literally overnight as prospectors rushed to Pennsylvania to seek their fortunes. As the amount of oil drilled increased, the problem of storing and transporting the oil became a problem. For barrel makers, known in those days as *coopers*, the fledgling industry provided a new outlet for their wooden casks. Barrels filled with the crude oil were often tied to rafts and floated down Oil Creek in an effort to get them to market.

In 1861 the world's first petroleum refinery, near Oil Creek, went on line producing primarily illuminating kerosene that was virtually odorless and smokeless. Railroads using flatcars transported the petroleum to refineries, and as the market grew, so did spur lines into the oil-producing region. In 1865 a railroad tank car was specifically designed for carrying crude oil.

That same year, the first oil pipeline was laid from Pithole City to the Oil Creek Railroad. It was two inches in diameter and thirty-two thousand feet long. In 1879 the first major pipeline was completed, stretching 110 miles across the Allegheny Mountains to Williamsport, Pennsylvania. By 1900 drillers were eyeing the possibility that petroleum could be found in salt domes along the Gulf of Mexico's coastline. And on January 10, 1901, in Gladys City, Texas, along the Spindletop ridge near Beaumont, a well drilled by Anthony F. Lucas struck oil, producing one hundred thousand barrels a day.

A second oil boom was on, and scenes from the Pennsylvania oil rush nearly fifty years earlier were replayed in the hundreds of small towns along the Texas Gulf of Mexico coast.

Discovering New Uses for Petroleum

By 1929, oil production in the United States had tripled from 1918 levels. It was during that year that American companies produced one billion barrels of oil for the first time in the short history of the petroleum industry.

By the spring of 2007, the United States was producing 5.2 million barrels per day of crude oil—one million barrels fewer than the decade before. Instead, we now import about 60 percent of our crude oil.

This oil is moved through more than two hundred thousand miles of pipelines that crisscross the continental United States, providing America with a stable and reliable source of fuel. This massive infrastructure, as critical to our way of life as highways, electric power lines, and cellular telephone towers, has been built underground not only for aesthetic considerations but also for environmental, cost, and security reasons, according to the American Petroleum Institute.

Another 180,000 miles of pipelines carry natural gas quietly, reliably, and efficiently throughout North America for heating, cooking, and other uses, according to the Interstate Natural Gas Association of America (www.ingaa.org).

Drake and Lucas had paved the way for the wholesale extraction of petroleum from the ground. Now inventors began to develop products that opened up a whole new market for crude oil and its products.

One of the first uses was in the internal combustion engine built in 1885–1886 by Karl Benz. The concept was improved on by Gottlieb Daimler, who developed an engine that used a lighter gasoline vapor. By 1894 Rudolf Diesel had designed the engine that bears his name today, an internal combustion engine ignited by the heat of compression rather than by a spark.

However, probably the most significant invention that changed the way Americans lived came in 1893 with the development of the first American car by Charles and Frank Duryea in Springfield, Massachusetts. In 1908 Henry Ford introduced his Model T. He subsequently perfected the mass production of automobiles, and America's love affair with the car had begun. This meant a completely new market for crude oil. Until the development and widespread use of the automobile, gasoline was considered a waste product. But as the number of automobiles grew, so did the number of gasoline stations across the country.

API's historical files note that the first "filling" station was opened in Seattle in 1907 by Standard Oil of California, which is now Chevron Company USA. The filling station included a hose that dispensed gasoline directly into the vehicle from an elevated tank. The first "drive-in" service station opened on December 1, 1913, in Pittsburgh, Pennsylvania.

According to the U.S. Department of Energy, there are now about 169,000 gasoline stations in the United States. Petroleum and its products, however, are used in many more ways. These include heating and cooling homes and factories, manufacturing goods, and fueling commercial and military aircraft, tractors, and railroads. New refining processes have led to the creation of thousands of new products, including bicycles, propane grills, crayons, plastic bottles, and laundry detergents. One can only imagine how different our lives would be today without these products, which have made many things so much easier.

Seven Sisters: Now There Are Four

U.S. entrepreneurs of the twentieth century realized the importance of petroleum and began to create companies to support this new form of energy. A study of the petroleum industry parallels the history and development of the United States and its emergence as a world leader in industry and technology.

From the industry's humble beginning grew seven oil companies that became known as the "seven sisters." Today, because of mergers and acquisitions, only four of the original seven remain.

No other name is as associated with those early years as that of John D. Rockefeller, who founded the Standard Oil Company of Ohio in 1870. This wealthy young man turned his few years of experience in the oil field into $1 million in cash and organized what was to be the first major oil company in the United States. Rockefeller quickly realized the importance of petroleum and, as the industry spread to other oil-producing states, so did his expansion into refineries and pipelines, as well as into overseas markets.

However, public and government outcry over his monopoly of the petroleum industry led, in part, to the passage of the Sherman Antitrust Act in 1890. A lawsuit was filed against the company under the new antitrust laws, but it was not until May 1911 that the United States Supreme Court ruled that Standard Oil must totally divest itself of its thirty-eight subsidiaries.

The largest of the subsidiaries was Standard Oil Company of New Jersey, which Rockefeller formed as a holding company to escape the tentacles of the antitrust laws. It later became known as Exxon, the largest oil company in the world. A second Rockefeller company was the Standard Oil Company of New York, which bought a Texas producing company called Magnolia. It merged with another firm called Vacuum and later became Mobil Oil. In November 1999 the two companies merged and are now known as ExxonMobil.

Eleven years before Rockefeller was ordered to dissolve his vast oil empire, he purchased a company and called it Standard Oil of

California, the forerunner of today's Chevron, USA. Another member of the early oil family was Gulf Oil Corporation, which was incorporated in New Jersey through the acquisition of the J. M. Guffey Petroleum Company and the Gulf Refining Company of Texas. These two companies were instrumental in the development of the prolific Spindletop field in Texas. Gulf Oil was acquired by Chevron in 1984.

The Texas Company—which later became Texaco—was another one of the sisters that had roots in the Texas oil patch but was founded by a Pennsylvania merchant. In 2001 Chevron and Texaco merged and became ChevronTexaco. In 2005 the name was changed to Chevron.

The last two sisters in the family were Shell Oil and British Petroleum, and both of these companies were founded in England. Even today they remain significant players in the worldwide energy business.

These seven companies, with the ability and finances to get petroleum out of the ground and get it to market, were to dominate the petroleum industry for decades to come. They, including other companies like ConocoPhillips (created in 2002 with the merger of Conoco and Phillips Petroleum Company) as well as many other smaller independent companies, are still active in the day-to-day search for petroleum.

By the mid-1970s, however, it was evident that the destinies of these large oil concerns were beginning to be inevitably shaped by a series of uncontrollable occurrences throughout the world, particularly in Middle Eastern countries—a scenario that hasn't changed much even well into the first decade of the twenty-first century.

Petroleum Industry of the Twenty-First Century

Since that first oil well was drilled in Pennsylvania, thousands of oil-field workers have dedicated their energies to improving the methods of getting the petroleum out of the ground. Out of the development of these new techniques grew a number of companies that provided services to the major oil companies. Thus, these firms that provided assistance to those drilling for oil came to be known as energy service companies.

Some of these same companies that broke new ground in the oil fields during the middle of the twentieth century have grown from small, family-owned firms to corporate giants with offices around the world. Names like Halliburton, Schlumberger, Baker–Hughes, Weatherford, and many others are heard each day during the course of drilling an oil well. Companies that explore and produce petroleum work hand in hand with service companies to find the petroleum that is so crucial to maintaining our standards of living.

While the first wells were drilled on land, there was a growing belief that oil reservoirs could be found in the vast waters off the shores of the continental United States. The first oil well to be drilled in water was in 1896 from a pier in Summerland, California. The first well to be drilled in open waters, however, occurred in 1937. The well, drilled by a joint agreement between the Superior Oil Company and Pure Oil Company, was off the coast of Louisiana in Gulf of Mexico waters.

Since that time, the coasts of Texas, Louisiana, Mississippi, Alabama, and Florida have become some of the world's most active areas for the exploration and production of oil and natural gas. And drilling operations are a common sight in western and eastern

Canada and from the icy waters of Europe's North Sea to the warm waters of the Mediterranean. Even today, drilling rigs are moving farther and farther away from land as new technologies are enabling drillers to search even deeper for petroleum.

Back on land, improved methods of getting the oil out of the ground are playing a substantial role in the energy future of the United States and Canada. These new techniques and equipment are showcased at oil exhibitions held periodically throughout the world in such locations as Houston and Midland/Odessa, Texas; Lafayette, Louisiana; Aberdeen, Scotland; Calgary, Canada; and Stavanger, Norway.

The search for petroleum is an exciting industry, providing unlimited daily challenges in a business whose technology is constantly developing and changing. However, the business is cyclical, and as of mid-2007, petroleum companies are seeking experienced personnel as North Americans realize the importance of a strong domestic energy industry and demand continues to grow.

While activity may be below the levels of the boom years of the late 1970s and early 1980s, there should be a steady need for experienced petroleum workers. So, for a person undecided on a career, the energy industry is expected to provide a multitude of jobs for years to come.

2

Petroleum Exploration

The search for petroleum, whether on land or in offshore waters, begins with the geologist—earth detectives who are sometimes called *petroleum geologists* or *exploration geologists* and who are trained to study, map, and interpret the many formations located beneath the earth's surface.

In the early days, geologists guessed where significant reservoirs of petroleum lay beneath the earth. Natural oil seeps were usually a good indication that petroleum lay beneath the surface. Through a lot of luck, and probably more good hunches than science, these geologists were able to find petroleum in those early years. They accomplished this by studying exposed creek beds, canyons, and railroad rights-of-way cuts for clues of what might lie beneath the surface.

As the methods of drilling for oil improved, the methods of finding it become more scientific. Today's geologists, while still performing basically the same function, have at their disposal a wide range of tools and instruments used to accurately study and map underground rock formations.

Geologists use many sources of information to interpret their findings, including core samples, computers, seismic data, paleontology, and geochemistry. But no matter how advanced the method and equipment, the geologist still must learn to accurately interpret data that have been compiled and correlated on certain types of formations. And, because of the value of the information, a geologist must keep any findings confidential until the employing company can secure the lease to drill for petroleum.

After a geologist completes the basic research on a potential oil field, a petroleum, or exploration, geophysicist is consulted to get a more detailed picture of subsurface formations.

Today's geophysicists use a wide range of sophisticated tools. Many are derived from the early days of the oil field. The first instruments used by early geophysicists included the surface magnetometer, refraction seismograph, and torsion balance for gravimetric surveying. Later tools were the reflection seismographs, gravimeters, and airborne magnetometers.

One of the most common methods that is used in today's energy industry—sometimes called the *oil patch*—is *seismology*, the study of the earth's tremors. This procedure involves making sound waves, called *seismic waves*, on the surface of the earth. The waves may be made by controlled explosives; vibrators; dropped heavy weights; or compressed gases, which produce bursts of energy using compressed air or propane. Once the waves penetrate the earth's crust, they reflect from subsurface rock layers back to the surface, where they are then recorded. Instruments such as a seismometer pick up the signals and record the waves on magnetic tape and on sensitized paper.

Other equipment includes the seismometer group recorder, which records the information on tape and helps eliminate noise and distortions that earlier methods could not overcome. Most of the recorded seismic data is transferred to computers, where various types of maps and cross sections are constructed. Radar also is used to examine potential oil-bearing areas when the land is covered by forests or clouds.

Another popular method is the stratigraphic test well, where a core sample is drilled in an area that may hold promise. This borehole sample is studied by geologists and paleontologists for traces of oil and gas and for fossils that might indicate the ages of the various rock strata.

While the methods used in searching for petroleum have vastly improved, oil companies continue to develop new and better techniques, including the increasing use of satellite imagery. Computers can now visually enhance seismic data that previously was pictured as squiggly lines and varying shades of darkness. With a few clicks of the mouse, underground formations now can be manipulated to add color, and specific target zones can be magnified for closer inspection.

Most oil companies use this 3-D technology to help drillers determine exactly where a well should be drilled. In older oil fields, the technology can also pinpoint pockets of oil that were missed using other technology.

The use of 3-D technology means that companies can make a quicker, more strategic decision about whether to drill a new oil field or whether there is more oil to be recovered in an old oil field.

Geoscientists

There are many job opportunities within the exploration field in both the private and government sectors. Petroleum companies are primarily interested in persons whose backgrounds are in sedimentation, paleontology, stratigraphy, geophysics, structural geology, or a related discipline.

The following information is from the 2006–2007 U.S. Department of Labor's *Occupational Outlook Handbook* (www.bls.gov/oco). This website is the primary source for most of the occupations, salaries, working conditions, and the outlook for future employment and will be frequently cited throughout this book.

Geoscientists study the composition, structure, and other physical aspects of the earth. With the use of sophisticated instruments and by analyzing the composition of the earth and water, geoscientists study the earth's geologic past and present. Many geoscientists are involved in searching for adequate supplies of natural resources such as groundwater, metals, and petroleum, while others work closely with environmental and other scientists in preserving and cleaning up the environment.

Geoscientists usually study, and are subsequently classified into, one of several closely related fields of geoscience. *Geologists* study the composition, processes, and history of the earth. They try to find out how rocks were formed and what has happened to them since their formation. They also study the evolution of life by analyzing plant and animal fossils. *Geophysicists* use the principles of physics, mathematics, and chemistry to study not only the earth's surface, but also its internal composition; ground and surface waters; atmosphere; oceans; and magnetic, electrical, and gravitational forces.

Oceanographers use their knowledge of geology and geophysics, in addition to biology and chemistry, to study the world's oceans and coastal waters. *Geological oceanographers* and *geophysical oceanographers* study the topographic features and the physical makeup of the ocean floor. Their knowledge can help companies find oil and gas off coastal waters.

Numerous specialties that further differentiate the type of work geoscientists do fall under the two major disciplines of geology and geophysics, according to the *Occupational Outlook Handbook*. For example, *petroleum geologists* map the subsurface of the ocean or land as they explore the terrain for oil and gas deposits. They use sophisticated geophysical instrumentation and computers to interpret geological information. *Engineering geologists* apply geologic principles to the fields of civil and environmental engineering, offering advice on major construction projects and assisting in environmental remediation and natural hazard-reduction projects.

Sedimentologists study the nature, origin, distribution, and alteration of sediments, such as sand, silt, and mud. These sediments may contain oil, gas, coal, and many other mineral deposits. *Paleontologists* study fossils found in geological formations to trace the evolution of plant and animal life and the geologic history of the earth. *Stratigraphers* examine the formation and layering of rocks to understand the environment in which they were formed.

Geoscientists can spend a large part of their time in the field identifying and examining rocks, studying information collected by remote sensing instruments in satellites, conducting geological surveys, constructing field maps, and using instruments to measure the earth's gravity and magnetic field. They often perform seismic studies, which involve bouncing energy waves off buried layers of rock, to search for oil and gas or to understand the structure of the subsurface layers. In laboratories, geologists and geophysicists examine the chemical and physical properties of specimens. They study fossil remains of animal and plant life or experiment with the flow of water and oil through rocks.

Working Conditions

Some geoscientists spend the majority of their time in an office, but many others divide their time between fieldwork and office or laboratory work, according to the *Occupational Outlook Handbook*. Work at remote field sites is common. Many geoscientists often take field trips that involve physical activity. Geoscientists in the field may work in warm or cold climates and in all kinds of weather. In their research, they may dig or chip with a hammer, scoop with a net, and carry equipment in a backpack. Oceanographers may spend considerable time at sea on academic research ships. Fieldwork often requires working long hours. Geologists frequently travel to remote field sites by helicopter or four-wheel-drive vehicles and cover large areas on foot.

An increasing number of exploration geologists and geophysicists work in foreign countries, sometimes in remote areas and under difficult conditions. Travel often is required to meet with prospective clients or investors.

Employment

According to the *Occupational Outlook Handbook*, geoscientists in the United States held about twenty-eight thousand jobs in 2004. Many more held geoscience faculty positions in colleges and universities but were classified as college and university faculty. About 20 percent worked for oil and gas extraction companies. In 2004, state agencies such as state geological surveys and state departments of conservation employed about thirty-six hundred geoscientists. Another twenty-nine hundred worked for the federal government, including geologists, geophysicists, and oceanographers, mostly within the U.S. Department of the Interior for the U.S. Geological Survey (USGS) and within the U.S. Department of Defense. About 5 percent of geoscientists were self-employed, most as consultants to industry or government.

Training, Other Qualifications, and Advancement

A bachelor's degree is adequate for a few entry-level positions, but most geoscientists need at least a master's degree in general geology or earth science. A master's degree also is the minimum educational requirement for most entry-level research positions in private industry, federal agencies, and state geological surveys. A Ph.D. degree is necessary for most high-level research and college teaching positions.

Many colleges and universities offer a bachelor's or higher degree in a geoscience. In 2005 more than a hundred universities offered accredited bachelor's degree programs in geoscience, about eighty universities had master's degree programs, and about sixty offered doctoral degree programs. Traditional geoscience courses emphasizing classical geologic methods and topics, such as mineralogy, petrology, paleontology, stratigraphy, and structural geology, are important for all geoscientists. Persons studying physics, chemistry, biology, mathematics, engineering, or computer science may also qualify for some geoscience positions if their course work includes study in geology or natural sciences.

Computer skills are essential for prospective geoscientists; students who have experience with computer modeling, data analysis and integration, digital mapping, remote sensing, and geographic information systems will be the most prepared entering the job market. Knowledge of the Global Information System (GIS) and Global Positioning System (GPS) has also become essential. Some employers seek applicants with field experience, so a summer internship may be beneficial to prospective geoscientists.

Geoscientists must have excellent interpersonal skills because they usually work as part of a team with other geoscientists and with environmental scientists, engineers, and technicians. Strong oral and written communication skills are important because writing technical reports and research proposals, as well as communicating research results to others, are important aspects of the work. Because many jobs require foreign travel, knowledge of a second language is becoming an important attribute to employers. Geoscientists must be inquisitive, able to think logically, and capable of complex analytical thinking, including spatial visualization and the ability to develop comprehensive conclusions often from sparse data. Those involved in fieldwork must have physical stamina.

Geoscientists often begin their careers in field exploration or as research assistants or technicians in laboratories or offices. They are given more difficult assignments as they gain experience. Eventually, they may be promoted to project leader, program manager, or some other management or research position.

Job Outlook

Although employment growth will vary by occupational specialty, overall employment of geoscientists in the United States is expected to grow more slowly than average (0 to 8 percent) for all occupations through 2014, according to the *Occupational Outlook Handbook*. However, due to the relatively low number of qualified geoscience graduates and the large number of expected retirements, opportunities are expected to be good in most areas of geoscience.

In Canada, work prospects for physical scientists, including geologists, are rated fair, according to Service Canada. The employment growth rate also will probably be close to the average. Although the retirement rate will likely be average, the number of retiring workers should contribute to job openings.

Graduates with a master's degree may have the best opportunities. Those with a Ph.D. who wish to become college and university faculty or to do advanced research may face competition. There are few openings for graduates with only a bachelor's degree in geoscience, but these graduates may find excellent opportunities as high school science teachers. They also can become science technicians or enter a wide variety of related occupations.

Few opportunities for geoscientists are expected in federal or state government, mostly because of budgetary constraints at key agencies, such as the United States Geological Survey and the trend among governments toward contracting out to consulting firms. However, departures of geoscientists who retire or leave the government for other reasons will result in some job openings over the next decade.

In recent years, a growing worldwide demand for oil and gas and for new exploration and recovery techniques—particularly in deep water and in previously inaccessible sites in Alaska and the Gulf of Mexico—has returned some stability to the petroleum industry. Growth in this area, though, will be limited due to increasing efficiencies in finding oil and gas. Geoscientists who speak a foreign language and who are willing to work abroad should enjoy the best opportunities, as the need for energy, construction materials, and a broad range of geoscience expertise grows in developing nations.

Job growth is expected within management, scientific, and technical consulting services. Demand will be spurred by a continuing emphasis on the need for energy, environmental protection, responsible land management, and water-related issues. Management, scientific, and technical consulting services have increased their hiring of many geoscientists in recent years due to increased government contracting and also in response to the demand for professionals to provide technical assistance and management plans to corporations. During periods of economic recession, geoscientists may be laid off. Especially vulnerable to layoffs are those in consulting and, to a lesser extent, workers in government. Employment for those working in the production of oil and gas, however, will be largely dictated by the cyclical nature of the energy sector and changes in government policy.

Earnings

Median annual earnings of geoscientists in the United States were $68,730 in May 2004. The middle 50 percent earned between $49,260 and $98,380; the lowest 10 percent earned less than $37,700 and the highest 10 percent more than $130,750. In Canada, hourly wages are C$29.23, and the rate of wage growth is close to the average, according to Service Canada.

According to the National Association of Colleges and Employers, beginning salary offers in July 2005 for graduates with bachelor's degrees in geology and related sciences averaged $39,365 a year.

The petroleum, mineral, and mining industries are vulnerable to recessions and to changes in oil and gas prices, among other factors, and usually release workers when exploration and drilling slow down. Consequently, they offer higher salaries but less job security than other industries.

Related Occupations

A petroleum geologist or a geophysicist who is responsible for analyzing and interpreting the information gathered usually heads exploration operations. Other geological specialists also may be involved in exploration activities, including paleontologists, who study fossil remains to locate oil; mineralogists, who study physical and chemical properties of mineral and rock samples; stratigraphers, who determine the rock layers most likely to contain oil and natural gas; and photogeologists, who examine and interpret aerial photographs of land surfaces. Also, exploration parties may include surveyors and drafters, who assist in surveying and mapping.

Some geologists and geophysicists work in district offices of oil companies or contract exploration firms, where they prepare and study geological maps and analyze seismic data. These scientists also may analyze samples from test drillings.

Other workers involved in exploration are geophysical prospectors. They lead crews consisting of gravity and seismic prospecting observers, who operate and maintain electronic seismic equipment; and scouts, who investigate the exploration, drilling, and leasing activities of other companies to identify promising areas to explore and lease.

Also, some physicists, chemists, atmospheric scientists, biological scientists, and environmental scientists and hydrologists—as well as mathematicians, computer systems analysts, computer scientists, and database administrators—perform related work both in the exploration and extraction of petroleum and natural gas and in activities having to do with the environment.

Companies that provide equipment and support services to those looking for petroleum also offer an abundance of opportunities. Additional opportunities are covered in Chapter 7.

Leasing Lands

Before any drilling, exploration, or production can take place on any land suspected of being a good oil prospect, the mineral rights must be secured from the property owner. This often complex but critical job is known as *leasing* and is the duty of a *landman*. (The job is not exclusive to men.) The American Association of Landmen (www.landman.org) describes a landman as someone who negotiates deals and trades with other companies and individuals, drafts contracts (and administers their compliance), acquires leases, and ensures compliance with governmental regulations.

Another name for a landman is a *right-of-way agent*. The *Directory of Occupational Titles* (www.occupationalinfo.org) describes a right-of-way agent as someone who negotiates with property owners and public officials to secure purchase or lease of land and right of way for utility lines, pipelines, and other construction projects. The agent determines roads, bridges, and utility systems that must be maintained during construction and negotiates with landholders for access routes and restoration of roads and surfaces. The agent might also examine public records to determine ownership and property rights and may also be required to know property law.

Independent field landmen serve clients on a contract basis and are generally the industry's contact with the public as they research courthouse records to determine ownership and prepare necessary reports, locate mineral/land owners and negotiate oil and gas leases and various other agreements with them, obtain necessary curative documents, and conduct surface inspections before drilling.

Independent land consultants serve clients on a contract basis, and much effort is directed to due diligence examinations required in the purchase and sale of companies and properties.

Landmen, who are specifically concerned with the legal rights to any hydrocarbons found beneath the subsoil, must deal primarily with two kinds of properties: public (owned by the government) and private (owned by an individual or corporation). A third type of property is land owned by Native Americans. However, no matter who owns the property, a landman must be knowledgeable in the particular laws of the land as well as adept in negotiating a contract satisfactory to all parties involved.

Leasing Private Lands

While a private landowner has the right to search for and remove any minerals from his or her own property, most have neither the finances nor the expertise to do so. Therefore, a landowner might decide to lease or sell all or part of his or her land rights to someone else. The primary function of a landman, then, is to search the title of the property, review the company's anticipated operations with the owners, negotiate signatures to the mineral lease, and have the contract recorded with the correct legal entity.

Most of the time the landman will begin negotiations with property owners after the geological work has been done. But in some instances, the leasing process begins prior to beginning the geophysical work. This usually happens when property is located in an extremely promising area where successful, producing wells have been drilled. Either way, the landman stays in constant contact and continues to work closely with the geologist and/or geophysicist.

A landman can offer a private landowner three options on his or her land: a lease interest, mineral interest, or royalty interest.

In an oil and gas lease, a written agreement is made between the landowner and the oil or gas company. This contract, usually written for a specific number of years, gives the company exclusive rights to enter the land, prospect for petroleum, and drill and remove any petroleum found there. In return, the landowner is given an initial bonus for agreeing to lease the land. Additionally, he or she gets a yearly rental fee based on how much acreage was leased. And, if the land does produce oil and gas, the landowner shares in the production in a form of compensation called royalty payments. The property owner can continue to use the surface of the land, as long as it does not interfere with the company's operations.

In a mineral interest option, a property owner can either sell the rights to some or all of his or her minerals, or sell the land and keep some or all of the mineral interests. This is where the job of a landman becomes more specialized and complicated, as the rights of either property owner may vary from state to state.

The last option a landman can offer a property owner is called royalty interest. This means a landowner agrees to transfer only the rights to the proceeds from the minerals.

The job of a landman is not only extremely important but very involved as well. There are many variations of lease options to negotiate and federal, state, and local laws to follow. A landman must be well versed in all of them.

Leasing Federal Lands in the United States and Canada

The federal government and Native American tribes own land in the United States that contains some of the country's most abundant oil and gas resources. This land is located onshore, as well as offshore in U.S. waters on the Outer-Continental Shelf (OCS).

The U.S. Geological Survey and the U.S. Department of Interior's Minerals Management Service (MMS) estimate that approximately 80 percent of the nation's oil—102 billion barrels—and nearly 60 percent of natural gas potentially are recoverable beneath federal lands and coastal waters.

The MMS is responsible for these resources and handles leasing the rights to private companies for the purpose of exploring and developing oil and gas. In return, the companies pay the federal government for the lease, as well as a royalty on the oil and gas they produce from the lease.

According to the MMS, annual revenues from federal onshore and offshore (OCS) mineral leases are one of the federal government's largest sources of non-tax income. In 2005, the MMS collected $7.7 billion in oil and gas royalties. The bulk of this ($5.5 billion) came from offshore production, with natural gas production generating 60 percent of the royalty revenue. For federal onshore lands, gas production generated more than 75 percent of the over $2 billion in royalties. The MMS also collected more than $750 million in bonus bids (for new leases), rental payments (to maintain the right to develop the lease in the future), and other revenues to bring the total federal revenues collected by MMS from oil and gas leasing and production on government lands to approximately $9.3 billion. In addition, Indian lands, separate from federal onshore lands, generated more than $340 million in revenues for Indian tribes and allottees.

The most visible types of federal land sales are the offshore lease sales for acreage located in the OCS. The MMS publishes the sale announcement at least one month in advance in the government's *Federal Register*.

Land owned by federal or state governments is usually acquired through a competitive bidding process involving numerous and specific rules and regulations. Federal onshore leasing is conducted through both competitive and noncompetitive methods. Prior to the date of the sale, companies submit sealed bids for the tracts, which normally have a five-year term. If the company whose bid was accepted does not conduct initial exploration operations as specified in the lease, the acreage reverts to the federal government, and the company loses the money paid to purchase the tracts.

Petroleum companies that do not own acreage in a certain offshore tract may try to participate in a *farm-in*. This means that the company would share an existing lease held by another company and be responsible for some or all of the cost of drilling a well. In return, the company would get a specified interest in the acreage. The opposite of a farm-in is a *farm-out*. In this type of leasing arrangement, a company already holding acreage would take on and pay drilling partners to explore certain portions of its holdings.

Whatever type of leasing arrangement is used, companies bid only on tracts where extensive geological tests have been conducted and analyzed and the prospects for a large find are possible.

The cost of drilling one offshore well continues to be in the millions of dollars. And, as the petroleum industry continues its quest for new oil frontiers, new technology is being applied to wells that are being drilled deeper, farther from land, and in even more remote locations far from the comforts of civilization.

How royalties (and other revenue) are distributed depends on the classification of the land from which the oil and gas were produced, according to the American Petroleum Institute. The distribution of royalties from onshore lands depends on whether they are public domain lands, acquired lands, or Alaska Native lands.

In general, MMS distributes the revenues it collects from oil and gas leasing and production on government lands to three main recipients: the U.S. Treasury, which receives more than half; the Land and Water Conservation Fund, which receives $900 million;

and the individual states. In 2005, states received about $1.3 billion from oil and gas activities on federal lands; more than $1 billion of this was from oil and gas royalties.

In Canada, *crown land* is the term that is used to describe land owned by the federal or provincial governments, according to *The Canadian Encyclopedia*. Authority for control of these public lands rests with the crown, hence their name. Less than 11 percent of Canada's land is in private hands; 41 percent is federal crown land, and 48 percent is provincial crown land. The Yukon Territory, Northwest Territories, and the territory of Nunavut (established in 1999) are administered on behalf of Canada by Indian and Northern Affairs Canada through the Territorial Lands Act and Public Lands Grants Act.

Surface and subsurface rights to the mineral, energy, forest, and water resources may be leased to private enterprise, a very important source of government income in Canada. National and provincial parks, Indian reserves, federal military bases, and provincial forests are the largest and most visible allocations of crown land.

Working as a Landman or Leasing Agent

The term *landman* is most likely a throwback to the early days in the oil field when few women, if any, were employed in the fledgling business. However, in today's oil patch (and in this book), the term is applicable to either gender.

Getting property owners to agree to have their land drilled and produced was, in fact, one of the first career opportunities in the petroleum industry that became available to women. Today, it continues to be a source of employment for women who have learned the art of negotiating and closing a deal.

As mentioned earlier in this chapter, landmen who work for major oil companies are sometimes called *land agents* or *right-of-way agents*. But whatever their titles may be, their ultimate responsibility remains the same: to secure the rights to explore, drill, and produce on tracts of land or the ocean bottom that earth scientists believe to be promising.

Training, Other Qualifications, and Advancement

Some colleges, primarily in the energy-producing states of Texas, Louisiana, and Oklahoma, and in Canada, offer degrees in petroleum land management. Some companies prefer land agents who have a law degree, since they sometimes negotiate exploration or development contracts with other producers. Or they arrange farm-in or farm-out agreements.

A natural progression from a land agent's job is a career in the company's legal affairs or general management departments.

Job Outlook

Many right-of-way agents work for companies that are subcontracted by larger companies for specific projects, which could require temporary relocation closer to the project site. Some landmen and geologists may be interested in the challenge of owning their own company. However, before setting out on your own, it would be wise to check with other professionals in the field in your particular part of the country. Because of the cyclical nature of the petroleum industry, it may be more prudent to remain in the security of a company rather than taking the risk of going out on your own. Trends in your particular area of specialization also may be checked out with the associations, schools, and organizations listed in the back of the book.

Job titles, responsibilities, and salaries vary by company, agency, and from state to state. For salary information, you can check out such sites as www.hotjobs.com, www.careerbuilder.com, www.monster.com, www.salary.com, or www.allbusiness.com.

3

Drilling Wells

Although the methods of determining where the most promising pockets of hydrocarbons are located have vastly improved since the days of Colonel Drake, the only sure way to find out is to actually drill a well.

Drilling an exploratory oil or gas well is costly, and detailed planning goes into a drilling program before the first hole is ever punched. There are three types of exploratory wells: those drilled to find the limits of an oil- or gas-bearing formation, those drilled in search of a new productive formation in an area that already contains commercial wells, and new field *wildcats*, those exploratory wells drilled where neither oil nor natural gas have been found before.

The cost of drilling one wildcat well is in the millions of dollars, depending, of course, on where the well is drilled and how deep it will be drilled. A company can absorb all of the costs of drilling a wildcat well, or if a company is incorporated, it can be financed from the sale of company stock. An operator may strike a deal with other companies, even with competitors, to share the risks—and rewards—if the well is successful.

Most of the early wells were quite shallow. Remember the Drake well, which was sixty-nine and a half feet deep and took fewer than fifteen days to drill? Today's wells are drilled to an average depth of nearly five thousand feet. Many more go beyond fifteen thousand feet.

To date, the world's deepest measured *extended-reach* drilled well was drilled in May 2007 by ExxonMobil's Russian subsidiary on Sakhalin Island, near Siberia, and it was drilled to a measured depth of 37,016 feet (11,282 meters) or more than seven miles.

The deepest *vertical* oil drilling record is still held by the Russians. In 1970, they began drilling on the Kola Peninsula in the northwest portion of the Soviet Union. When drilling stopped in 1994, the hole was more than seven miles deep (12,262 meters), making it by far the deepest hole ever drilled.

Obviously, the deeper a well is drilled, the longer it takes to drill and the higher the cost. As the price of oil increased in the late 1970s and the early 1980s, so did the cost of drilling. Since 1992, America's oil and natural gas industry has invested more than $1 trillion in exploration, development, production, and distribution of oil and gas, according to the American Petroleum Institute (API).

In May 2007, there were about 1,850 rotary drilling rigs operating in the United States. The all-time high was 4,530 on December 28, 1981, and the record low was 488 on April 23, 1999, according to Baker Hughes, an oil field service company that has been tracking the numbers for decades.

Although most wells are drilled vertically, some operators use the directional drilling technique. This method of drilling allows several wells to be drilled from one location. This is an advantage, especially offshore, where the cost of one platform may run into the millions of dollars.

Most of the explorers who drill new oil and natural gas wells in the United States are the smaller drillers of the industry, called *independents*. An independent can be an individual, partnership, or public corporation.

At the peak of the oil boom there were about fifteen thousand independents. Today, there are about five thousand of these wildcatters who drill wells that are historically successful only one out of five times. The other four wells, on the average, are dry holes.

A typical independent does not own refineries or gasoline service stations. The independent runs his or her own business, calling the shots on whether to drill. Although the names of independent drillers may not be as familiar as those of the larger companies—known as *majors*—their role in the exploration and production of new oil and gas reserves is of great significance.

Here are some facts about independent producers from the Independent Petroleum Association of America (www.ipaa.org):

- America's thousands of independent oil and natural gas producers and service companies operate in thirty-three states and the coastal waters offshore.
- Independents derive their income primarily from the sale of oil and natural gas they discover and produce in their operations. This is commonly called the *upstream* segment of the industry.
- Independent producers develop 90 percent of domestic oil and gas wells, produce 68 percent of domestic oil, and produce 82 percent of domestic natural gas.
- A recent analysis has shown that independent producers are investing 150 percent of their domestic cash flow back into domes-

tic oil and natural gas development and are borrowing funds to enhance already aggressive efforts to find and produce more energy.

• Independent producers range in size from large publicly traded companies to small mom-and-pop family businesses that drill only a few wells each year.

• Most independents have fewer than twenty employees. Yet, collectively, independent producers are the key to future domestic energy exploration and production.

Independents sell their crude oil to refineries, which in turn market the refined products through their own outlets or through those of independent marketers. Natural gas reserves discovered and produced by independents are sold at the wellhead to natural gas pipelines, which in turn sell it to local gas utilities for distribution to consumers.

Major petroleum companies can rely on other sources of revenue from their companies when oil and natural gas prices fall below a profitable level. Independent producers, however, live and die by the price they receive at the wellhead.

Drilling a Well on Land

Once an independent or major company decides to drill a well on land, it first must select a well site that is easily accessible, as level as possible, and located so the drilling process will have as little effect on the surrounding environment as possible. The company, known as the *operator*, then invites drilling contractors, those companies that own and operate rigs, to bid on the job. Once the job is awarded and all costs negotiated, a contract is signed between the operator and drilling contractor.

Personnel who will be involved with the drilling are brought in, and the site is cleared and leveled in preparation for placement of the drilling rig. In some cases, turnarounds and access roads built of planks (called *board runs*) are built, while support facilities are brought in for the crew. If the area is not easily accessible, heavy lift helicopters are used to bring in the equipment. The property will be altered with this work. However, laws and regulations require that the change be minimal and repairable. The land must be restored to its natural state after drilling.

Large amounts of water are needed during land-drilling operations. If a stream, river, or other suitable source of water is nearby, pumps and a waterline are installed to bring water from that source to the drill site. If this source of water is not readily available, a water well is drilled.

Because of regulations and an increased awareness of the environment by oil companies, there has been more care taken when disposing of materials considered potentially hazardous to the area. Part of the preparation includes digging an earthen pit, which is then lined with plastic. This pit is used to collect used or unneeded nontoxic drilling materials. After the well is drilled, the pit is covered and leveled.

If the well is located in an ecologically sensitive area, little, if any, waste is dumped at the site. Trucks are used to transport the material to locations that have been approved for disposal.

Drilling a Well Offshore

Although the concept of drilling an offshore well is basically the same as drilling one on land, there are very different situations that must be dealt with when drilling in great depths of water.

After the drilling contractor is awarded the contract, preparations of the offshore site are made. Buoys are set to mark the spot where the operators want to drill. Some offshore rigs sit atop platforms. Therefore, these rigs must be transported from land to barges to the site. To be moved, the rig is usually divided into sections, called *packages*, which are hoisted individually by crane onto the barge. The rig is then reassembled on the platform. This requires precise planning, since all supplies needed to rig up will have to be brought along on the trip.

Types of Rigs

While all onshore wells are basically drilled the same, the type of offshore well to be drilled determines the kind of rig that will be used. Depending on the depth of the water, climatic conditions of the area, and the costs involved, any one of five kinds of mobile offshore drilling units (MODU) can be used to drill exploratory wells.

There are two basic types of offshore drilling rigs: those that can be moved from place to place, allowing for drilling in multiple locations; and those rigs that are permanently placed. Moveable rigs are often used for exploratory purposes because they are much cheaper to use than permanent platforms. Once large deposits of hydrocarbons have been found, a permanent platform is built to allow their extraction.

- **Drill barges.** An inland drilling barge, used in shallow and inland waters, is a drilling rig mounted on a barge and towed by a tug. Any movement of the barge must be made under the power of another vessel. Barges also house equipment, supplies, and crew quarters, although other services associated with drilling a well are usually furnished from other barges or vessels.

• **Drill ships.** Drill ships are exactly as they sound: ships that are designed to carry out drilling operations. These boats are specially rigged to transport drilling platforms out to deep-sea locations. In addition to all of the equipment normally found on a large ocean ship, a typical drill ship will have a drilling platform and derrick located on the middle of its deck. Also, drill ships contain a hole (or *moonpool*), extending right through the ship and down through the hull, which allows for the drill string to extend through the boat and down into the water.

Drill ships are frequently used to drill in very deep water, which can often be quite turbulent. Drill ships use what are known as *dynamic positioning* systems and are equipped with electric motors on the undersides of their hulls that are capable of propelling ships in any direction. These motors are integrated into a ship's computer system, which uses satellite positioning technology, in conjunction with sensors located on the drilling template, to ensure that the ship is directly above the drill site at all times.

• **Jack-up rigs.** Jack-up rigs are similar to drill barges, with one difference. Once a jack-up rig is towed to the drilling site, three or four *legs* are lowered until they rest on the sea bottom. This allows the working platform to rest above the surface of the water, as opposed to a floating barge. However, jack-up rigs are suitable for shallower waters, as extending these legs down too deeply would be impractical. Because the working platforms are elevated above the water, these rigs are typically safer to operate than drilling barges.

• **Submersible rigs.** One of the oldest types of rigs used for exploration are the submersible rigs. Their design probably came from the first offshore rigs, which were sunken barges that were secured in place by wooden pilings. Submersible rigs have an upper level that houses the crew and working area and a lower level—the hull—that sits on the bottom while drilling. The hull is pumped out and floated to move the rig to a new location.

Submersibles drill in shallow water of thirty to forty feet, although newer units are able to drill to nearly one hundred feet or more. Once exploration is completed, it is moved to a new site.

- **Semisubmersible rigs.** Semisubmersible rigs are the most common type of offshore drilling rigs, combining the advantages of submersible rigs with the ability to drill in deep water. Semisubmersible rigs work on the same principle as submersible rigs—through the inflating and deflating of their lower hulls. The main difference with a semisubmersible rig, however, is that when the air is let out of the lower hull, the rig does not submerge to the seafloor. Instead, the rig is partially submerged and still floats above the drill site. When drilling, the lower hull, which is filled with water, provides stability to the rig.

Semisubmersible rigs are held in place by huge anchors, each weighing about ten tons. These anchors, combined with the submerged portion of the rig, ensure that the platform is stable and safe enough to be used in turbulent offshore waters. Semisubmersible rigs can be used to drill in much deeper water—up to ten thousand feet—than the other rigs described.

After the existence of hydrocarbons is confirmed, developmental drilling may be planned. These locations are sometimes drilled from a rig sitting atop a fixed offshore platform that was constructed in an onshore fabrication yard. These platforms must be designed and constructed to withstand the extreme forces of nature, such as hurricanes in the Gulf of Mexico, icy winds in the Arctic

Sea, or earthquakes in the Pacific Ocean. Once constructed, they are loaded on barges and towed out to a location. Once at a site, they are lowered to the bottom and securely anchored to the seafloor with pilings, which are driven deep into the earth. Huge cranes lift the rig packages from the barge to the platform, where several wells can be drilled by sliding a movable derrick to drilling slots built into the platform.

Since the first platform was installed in the twenty-foot waters of the Gulf of Mexico in 1947, thousands of fixed platforms have been placed throughout the world's prolific offshore areas. About half of all offshore structures in the world are in the Gulf of Mexico, where some have been placed in more than one thousand feet of water. Energy production in the Gulf of Mexico reached 1.6 million barrels of oil per day in May 2005 and is expected to exceed 1.7 million barrels of oil per day in the next ten years, according to the U.S. Mineral Management Service.

About 150,000 full- and part-time employees work off the shores of the U.S. mainland in exploration, development, and production jobs in the Gulf of Mexico alone. Additional spending by contractors, vendors, and employees creates more than twice that number of jobs.

Components of a Drilling Rig

It is up to the contractor drilling the well to provide the proper equipment and personnel to operate a rig as agreed upon in the contract. The main function of a rotary drilling rig, the most common type of rig used, is to drill a well, or *make hole*, as it is called in the industry. All drilling rigs have four main components: power, hoisting, rotating, and circulation systems.

Power System

Most all rigs use a diesel-fueled internal combustion engine as their main source of power. A rig's engine is not unlike a car's engine, only much larger and much more powerful. Most rigs are powered by at least two engines that provide from five hundred to three thousand horsepower.

Hoisting System

This system is composed of five parts: The *hoist* is used to run the drill pipe in and out of the hole to change drill bits or run tools. This drill string (drill pipe and drill collars) must be lifted out of the well, disconnected, and racked back; the bit changed; and then run back in the hole. The *derrick* is designed to withstand extremely high winds with the racks full of pipe. The drilling line is wound around a revolving drum called the *drawworks*, which houses the main brake used to hold and stop the many pounds of pipe being raised and lowered into the well.

The *traveling block* and *crown block* are each a series of large pulleys through which the drill line travels. This system of multiple lines increases the hoisting ability of the drawworks.

Rotating System

This component is comprised of all the parts that extend from the swivel to the drill bit. All of the parts move, providing motion for the drill bit.

The *swivel* carries the weight of the drill string, permits it to rotate, and provides an opening for the circulating fluid. The *kelly* is a hollow, six-sided tube that helps keep the drill string moving vertically as it is lowered during drilling operations. Providing the torque to turn the drill stem and space for slips to hold the pipe is the *rotary table*. Mud is pumped through thirty-foot sections of *drill pipe* and *drill collars* to which are attached the *drill bit*, which is used to break up the formation. There are a variety of drill bits on the market, and what type is used depends upon the formation being drilled.

Circulation System

Drilling fluid, called *mud* in the petroleum business, is usually composed of a mixture of water, clay, weighting material, and a few chemicals. It is used to raise cuttings made by the bit and lift them to the surface for disposal. But more important, perhaps, is that it helps keep underground pressures in check. It is part of several safety measures used to protect workers from a blowout. This safety measure, as well as others, are covered later in this chapter. Fluid-circulating equipment and mud are major costs associated with drilling a well. Other equipment is needed to maintain the consistency of the drilling mud, as well as equipment for removing fine solids.

Drilling operations begin by attaching a bit to the drill string. This drill string passes through a turntable on the derrick floor, and as the pipe is lowered and rotated into the earth, the bit rotates and bores deeper and deeper into the ground. As the hole is drilled, new pipe is added. When drill bits become dull or break, the entire drill string must be pulled out, the bit changed, and the drill string run back into the hole. This process of removing, reconnecting, and then resuming drilling happens over and over again when a deep well is being drilled.

Safety While Working on a Drilling Rig

While developing technology has kept the number of blowouts to a minimum, there is still a large amount of danger associated with drilling a well. New employees are instructed in the proper safety rules and regulations of working on an offshore drilling rig. Specific duties also are assigned in case the rig has to be suddenly evacuated. Periodic safety drills are held, and all personnel must be familiar with escape routes.

Offshore rigs are equipped with a helipad for the use of helicopters to ferry crews on and off the rigs. It also can be used for evacuation purposes. Offshore rigs are equipped with survival capsules, and employees are instructed in how to properly board and launch them. Other offshore survival techniques are taught to workers, such as how to escape from a helicopter that has overturned in the water.

About two decades ago, numerous major oil companies contributed to the establishment of the Marine Survival Training Center, a facility built in conjunction with the University of Louisiana at Lafayette. It was built in response to Coast Guard regulations that went into effect in early 1989, requiring that several individuals on every offshore installation be trained in launching and navigating survival capsules. The center was the nation's first large-scale training facility for training personnel to operate the capsules. Instruction includes launching, piloting, and retrieving survival capsules, as well as using them in fire and hydrogen sulfide emergencies. Beginning January 2007, a new regulation required that all offshore personnel who work in the Gulf of Mexico must take a survival training course.

Some petroleum workers have been killed or injured when the well pressure is not controlled. This is called a *blowout*. However, improved drilling techniques and new equipment help monitor and control well-bore pressure. On both land and offshore rigs, a blowout preventer is installed under the rig floor. Valves to close the well can be controlled from a remote panel, should it become necessary. If a blowout is serious, rig workers are evacuated, and experienced wild-well fighters, such as the firm began by the legendary Red Adair, are called in to shut the well.

Opportunities in Drilling

The energy business is cyclical, and in mid-2007, there once again was a shortage of drilling personnel, similar to the experience in 1986 and again in 1998. Many experienced professional and technical workers gave up on this cyclical industry and moved on to other lines of work. The industry is facing another critical shortage in the next decade as experienced workers who remained in the industry are now ready to retire. This could provide opportunities for those who want to make the energy business a career.

Petroleum Engineers

Petroleum engineers search for reservoirs containing oil or natural gas. Once a petroleum field is discovered, they work with geologists and other specialists to understand the geologic formation and properties of the rock, determine the drilling methods to be used, and monitor drilling and production operations. They design equipment and processes to achieve the maximum profitable recovery of oil and gas.

Because only a small proportion of oil and gas in a reservoir flows out under natural forces, petroleum engineers develop and use various enhanced recovery methods. These include injecting water, chemicals, gases, or steam into an oil reservoir to force out more of the oil, and doing computer-controlled drilling or *fracturing* to connect a larger area of a reservoir to a single well. Even the best techniques in use today recover only a portion of the oil and gas in a reservoir, so petroleum engineers research and develop technology and methods to increase recovery and lower the cost of drilling and production operations.

Working Conditions

Petroleum engineers work in the office but also spend time at oil and gas exploration and production sites, where they monitor or direct operations or solve on-site problems. At times, deadlines or design standards may bring extra pressure to a job, requiring engineers to work longer than a forty-hour workweek.

Employment

In 2004, engineers in the United States held 1.4 million jobs, according to the 2006–2007 *Occupational Outlook Handbook*. Of that number, petroleum engineers held about sixteen thousand jobs, mostly in the petroleum industry and in closely allied fields.

Employers include major oil companies and hundreds of smaller, independent oil exploration, production, and service companies. Engineering consulting firms, government agencies, oil-field services companies, and equipment suppliers also employ petroleum engineers. Others work as independent consultants. A few are employed in the refining, transportation, and retail sectors of the oil and gas industry.

Most petroleum engineers work where oil and gas are found. Large numbers are employed in Texas, Oklahoma, Louisiana, and

California, including offshore sites. Many American petroleum engineers also work overseas in oil-producing countries. The largest number of engineers in Canada is found in Alberta and Ontario, according to Service Canada.

Training, Other Qualifications, and Advancement

A bachelor's degree in engineering is required for almost all entry-level engineering jobs, according to the 2006–2007 *Occupational Outlook Handbook.* Most engineering degrees are granted in electrical, electronics, mechanical, or civil engineering. However, engineers trained in one branch may work in related branches. This flexibility allows employers to meet staffing needs in new technologies and specialties in which engineers may be in short supply. It also allows engineers to shift to fields with better employment prospects or to those that more closely match their interests.

Most engineering programs involve a concentration of study in an engineering specialty, along with courses in both mathematics and the physical and life sciences. General courses not directly related to engineering, such as those in the social sciences or humanities, are also often a required component of programs. A design course, sometimes accompanied by a computer or laboratory class or both, is part of the curriculum of most programs.

In addition to the standard engineering degree, many colleges offer two- or four-year degree programs in engineering technology. These programs, which usually include various hands-on laboratory classes that focus on current issues in the application of engineering principles, prepare students for practical design and production work rather than for jobs that require more theoretical and scientific knowledge. Graduates of four-year technology programs may get jobs similar to those obtained by graduates with a bachelor's degree in engineering. Engineering technology graduates, however, are not qualified to register as professional engineers under the same terms as graduates with degrees in engineering. Some employers regard technology program graduates as having skills between those of a technician and an engineer.

About 364 colleges and universities offer bachelor's degree programs in engineering that are accredited by the Accreditation Board for Engineering and Technology (ABET), Inc., and about 226 colleges offer accredited programs in engineering technology. ABET accreditation is based on an examination of an engineering program's student achievement, program improvement, faculty, facilities, curriculum, and institutional commitment to certain principles of quality and ethics.

Although most institutions offer programs in the major branches of engineering, only a few offer programs in the smaller specialties. Also, programs of the same title may vary in content. For example, some programs emphasize industrial practices, preparing students for a job in industry; others are more theoretical and are designed to prepare students for graduate work. Therefore, students should investigate curriculums and check accreditations carefully before selecting a college.

Admissions requirements for undergraduate engineering schools include a solid background in mathematics (algebra, geometry, trigonometry, and calculus) and science (biology, chemistry, and physics), with courses in English, social studies, and the humanities. Bachelor's degree programs in engineering generally are designed to last four years, but many students find that it takes between four and five years to complete their studies. In a typical four-year college curriculum, the first two years are spent studying mathematics, basic sciences, introductory engineering, humanities, and social sciences. In the last two years, most courses are in engineering, usually with a concentration in one specialty. Some programs offer a general engineering curriculum; students then specialize on the job or in graduate school.

Some engineering schools and two-year colleges have agreements whereby the two-year college provides the initial engineering education, and the engineering school automatically admits students for their last two years. In addition, a few engineering schools have arrangements that allow students who spend three years in a liberal arts college studying pre-engineering subjects and two years in an engineering school studying core subjects to receive a bachelor's degree from each school. Some colleges and universities offer five-year master's degree programs. Some five-year or even six-year cooperative plans combine classroom study and practical work, permitting students to gain valuable experience and to finance part of their education.

All fifty states and the District of Columbia require licensure for engineers who offer their services directly to the public. Engineers who are licensed are called *professional engineers* (PE). This licensure generally requires a degree from an ABET-accredited engineering program, four years of relevant work experience, and successful completion of a state examination. Several states have imposed mandatory continuing education requirements for relicensure. Most states recognize licensure from other states, provided that the manner in which the initial license was obtained meets or exceeds their own licensure requirements. Many civil, electrical, mechanical, and chemical engineers are licensed PEs. Independent of licensure, various certification programs are offered by professional organizations to demonstrate competency in specific fields of engineering.

In Canada, the licensing of engineers is carried out by twelve provincial and territorial associations (*orders* in Québec) that set standards and regulate the profession, according to Engineers Canada, the national organization of the twelve provincial and territorial associations that regulate the practice of engineering in Canada and license the country's more than 160,000 professional engineers.

An engineering license is valid only within that jurisdiction. However, there is a mobility agreement among the provinces and territories regarding transfer of licenses.

Once registered, or licensed, as a member of a provincial or territorial association, engineers are known as professional engineers and are eligible to use the designation "P.Eng." ("ing." in Québec) after their name.

Before being accepted for registration and licensure, individuals normally are required to pass a series of examinations set by the licensing body in the province or territory where they intend to reside. They must also demonstrate sufficient communication skills in at least one of Canada's two official languages and have three or four years of acceptable engineering work experience, including one year of experience in a Canadian environment. For more information, go to www.engineerscanada.ca.

Engineers should be creative, inquisitive, analytical, and detail oriented. They should be able to work as part of a team and to communicate well, both orally and in writing. Communication abilities are important because engineers often interact with specialists in a wide range of fields outside engineering.

Beginning engineering graduates usually work under the supervision of experienced engineers and in large companies also may receive formal classroom or seminar-type training. As new engineers gain knowledge and experience, they are assigned more difficult projects with greater independence to develop designs, solve problems, and make decisions. Engineers may advance to become technical specialists or to supervise a staff or team of engineers and technicians. Some may eventually become engineering managers or enter other managerial or sales jobs.

Job Outlook

Petroleum engineers in the United States are expected to have a decline in employment through 2014 because most of the potential petroleum-producing areas in the United States already have been explored, according to the *Occupational Outlook Handbook.* Even so, favorable opportunities are expected for petroleum engineers because the number of job openings is likely to exceed the relatively small number of graduates. All job openings should result from the need to replace petroleum engineers who transfer to other occupations or leave the labor force. Petroleum engineers work around the world and, in fact, the best employment opportunities may be in other countries. Many foreign employers seek U.S.-trained petroleum engineers, and many U.S. employers maintain overseas branches.

Service Canada predicts the outlook for some engineers, including petroleum engineers, will continue to be fair because the employment growth rate will likely be above average and the number of retiring workers should contribute to job openings. However, the number of job seekers will likely exceed the number of jobs.

Earnings

Earnings for engineers vary significantly by specialty, industry, and education. Even so, as a group, engineers earn some of the highest average starting salaries among those holding bachelor's degrees.

According to a 2005 survey by the National Association of Colleges and Employers, the average starting salary for a petroleum engineer with a bachelor's degree in the United States was $61,516—the highest of all starting salaries of bachelor's degree graduates in engineering disciplines, according to the *Occupational Outlook Handbook*.

The *Occupational Outlook Handbook* notes that the median hourly earnings is $47.24 for petroleum engineers in the United States. According to Service Canada, hourly wages are C$32.31, and the rate of wage growth is close to the average.

Additional Jobs in the Drilling Sector

A large number of people are involved in directly drilling a well. A large drilling contractor may own fifty rigs, while smaller ones may own only a few. Larger contractors may have rigs operating all over the world. Usually, area or regional offices are set up in strategic locations where rigs may typically operate.

A regional manager, drilling superintendent, and drilling/production engineer usually are responsible for several rigs. They work in the regional office and keep in daily contact with the rig by telephone, radio, and e-mail.

Drilling/production engineers are responsible for planning, directing, and coordinating activities required to erect, install, and maintain equipment for exploratory or production drilling of oil and gas. They also may direct technical processes and analyses to resolve drilling problems and monitor and control operating costs and production efficiency. This position requires good administrative skills, knowledge of the business, deductive reasoning, and the ability to coordinate the work of others.

Working on the rig is a *toolpusher*, who is actually in charge of the work site. The toolpusher supervises and coordinates activities of workers engaged in drilling oil and gas wells in an area consisting of one or more well sites. He or she directs workers to erect, dismantle, and move drilling rigs; and instructs drilling crews to set up and operate power units and draw works and other drilling equipment.

The toolpusher plans delivery of drilling tools, fuel, water, and other supplies for use at the drill site; orders the type of drilling bits to be used according to type of strata encountered; and directs workers in mixing drilling mud and in circulating mud in the borehole and in the use of special drilling mud to prevent blowouts from gas pressure.

He or she also orders the installation of the *control head* (valve device) to control flow when the well begins to produce gas or oil; supervises operations at producing wells to maintain and regulate the flow of oil and natural gas; and performs other supervisory duties as needed.

Drilling operations are conducted around the clock in shifts called *tours* (pronounced *towers*). Offshore personnel generally work twelve-hour shifts, seven days on and seven days off. Onshore, the shifts are eight hours, and they generally work five days on, with two days off.

The head of each tour is a *driller*, who heads a crew comprised of a derrickman and three roughnecks. The driller's job is one of the most important on a rig and requires several years of experience. He or she is usually promoted to the driller's position after working several years each as a derrickman, floorman, and roustabout.

Drillers work closely with the toolpusher and company representative while carrying out the drilling program. A driller must be able to make quick decisions during drilling operations and, if a blowout or accident occurs, must calmly handle the emergency and administer first aid. A driller is also the crew's morale booster, as well as the person who sometimes assists with personnel recruitment.

A *derrickman* may be considered something of a daredevil. Attached with a safety belt about ninety feet above the drill floor, the derrickman racks the drill string as it is pulled from the well. He or she also handles the drill string when it goes back into the hole. In most cases, the derrickman is also responsible for the mud system and mud pumps. The danger of this job is compounded by high winds and, if an accident such as a blowout occurs, the derrickman may get caught up in the derrick.

Floormen, better known as *roughnecks*, perform most of the physical work during drilling operations. They are responsible for screwing and unscrewing the joints of pipe as they come out of the hole. They also must wash down and rack the pipe as it comes out, making it one of the dirtiest and greasiest jobs on a rig. Since they work outside and are unprotected from the elements, roughnecks must enjoy the outdoors and be able to adapt to the rigors of any climate.

Some drilling personnel begin their careers as *roustabouts*, those persons who assist with the drilling operations and perform general maintenance on a drilling rig.

Offshore rig workers live and work on offshore rigs during their shift, usually called "seven and seven." That means a rig worker will work seven straight days and then will be off seven days. Some overseas jobs call for "fourteen and fourteen" or "twenty-eight and twenty-eight" shifts. Land-rig personnel may live in trailers moved in near the well site or at other close quarters provided by the company. But whatever the work schedule, the rig workers, supplemented by personnel from service companies called in to perform certain operations, actually drill the well.

The opportunities for working on a drilling rig depend, of course, on the amount of drilling activity planned by major oil companies and independents. Salaries vary, dependent upon the level of activity in the industry and the number of experienced workers available.

According to the *Occupational Outlook Handbook*, 2004 median hourly earnings in the United States for some of these positions include: general and operations managers, $49.93; first-line supervisors/managers of construction trades and extraction workers, $27.44; petroleum pump-system operators, refinery operators, and gaugers, $23.52; rotary drill operators, oil and gas, $16.17; derrick operators, oil and gas, $15.26; roustabouts, oil and gas, $12.60; and helpers-extraction workers, $11.58.

More information can also be found at some of the specific energy-related employment websites listed in Appendix A.

4

Producing and Recovering Petroleum from the Ground

The cost to drill and produce petroleum is very expensive, especially in areas such as the Gulf of Mexico, where companies are venturing farther off the coast of the United States and are drilling deeper wells. Because the cost of drilling and producing a well is very expensive, producers must decide whether it will be profitable to bring the well into production.

It is the job of a petroleum engineer to plan and execute the following steps:

- Evaluate the formation
- Isolate the formation
- Stimulate the well
- Install production equipment

The production engineer will then optimize hydrocarbon production from existing wells through the use of chemical or mechanical stimulation. He or she also may be involved in reevaluating the method used to lift the oil and gas out of the reservoir or in sizing and selecting separation, handling, metering, and disposal equipment as part of the surface-treating facility.

To evaluate the formation requires the services of a *mud logger*, who monitors conditions below the surface while the well is being drilled. Using a microscope or ultraviolet light, the mud logger looks at cuttings made by the drill bit from the rock formation in the well below. From these cuttings, he or she is able to determine whether oil is present. Another tool used by the mud logger for the same purpose is a gas detection instrument.

A technique called *well-logging* also is used. A logging tool is lowered into the well and then slowly reeled back to the surface. As it is brought back up, the tool is able to measure the properties of the formations through which it has passed. Electric logs work by measuring and recording resistivity in the formations, while some logs use sound waves to help define the formations.

Another popular device measures the formation pressure as fluids enter the tool. Core samples also are used to determine the presence of hydrocarbons in the particular formation. Other methods use a radioactive source to define formations.

Completing a Well

If no hydrocarbons are present, or if an operator believes the cost would be prohibitive to produce the well, he or she may decide to seal off the well, using a number of methods collectively known as *plug and abandonment*. Government regulations require that both onshore and offshore well sites be cleared of all debris and wells sealed with cement plugs to prevent fluids from escaping from or entering into the well. Some areas require that the land surrounding onshore wells be replanted and reworked. In some cases, there is little evidence that a well had ever been drilled.

To prevent problems for commercial vessels, some offshore wells are plugged and cut off below the seafloor. However, in some coastal areas, abandoned offshore platforms are left in place or moved to another area to be used as artificial reefs. Fish and other sea creatures are attracted to the structures, thus providing a better than average sport fishing environment.

If a well looks promising and the price of oil or natural gas warrants it, operators sometimes go back and produce a well that has been plugged and abandoned.

Operators have a tough decision to make when deciding to produce a well, since the cost of bringing a well into production can be very expensive. If an operator determines that a well would be economically feasible to produce, he or she begins preparations for production. This is known as *completing a well.*

Pipe called *production casing* is set and cemented in the formation to isolate the *pay zone* (productive area). To get the well to flow up to the surface, a technique known as *perforating* is used. The most common method of perforating is to fire charges through the production casing and into the formation. This provides a means for the fluid to get into the well bore so the hydrocarbons can flow into it and up to the surface. A piece of equipment built with a series of arms and valves and called a *Christmas tree* is attached to the wellhead. This device controls the well and the flow of oil or gas into the gathering pipelines.

Different types of wells present different completion problems, and operators have alternate methods at their disposal for completing a well.

Recovering Petroleum from the Well

Scientists estimate that only about one-fourth of the oil in a reservoir is recovered by natural flow and pumping. Consequently, most wells need a little help in getting the oil to flow at a slow, steady rate.

Reservoir engineers are usually called in to make decisions about major development phases for a reservoir. They must select the method most economically beneficial to the reservoir by calculating the amount of recoverable oil and gas. Then they must determine the number of wells economically justified to recover those reserves. Specially designed computer programs are used to simulate future performance, allowing better decisions to be made about the reservoir.

One of the most common types of primary recovery methods used is the *artificial lift*, including the use of a pumping unit. This piece of equipment, sometimes called a *horse's head* because it looks like a gigantic rocking horse, is required for most wells when natural pressure diminishes. Another artificial lift technique used is the circulation of natural gas, which forces the oil to the surface. Special pumps also can be used to push the flow of oil through the well.

In more recent years, a variety of enhanced oil recovery methods have been used. *Enhanced oil recovery* (EOR) is a generic term for techniques used to increase the amount of oil that can be extracted from an oil field. It is estimated that through the use of EOR, 30 to 60 percent of the reservoir's original oil can be extracted, compared to 20 to 40 percent using primary and secondary recovery methods.

EOR techniques include the use of water flooding and chemical flooding, as well as thinning the oil by heating to make it flow easier. There are several types of recovery methods, but all center on injecting certain chemicals or gases that mix with the oil. *Thermal recovery* uses steam injection to thin thick crude oil, thereby making it easier to produce. Another method is called *fire flooding*. This is accomplished by starting a fire in the reservoir, which is fed by injected air.

Service and Maintenance

After production equipment is installed on a producing well, it must be periodically serviced to maintain or improve production. This is called *well servicing*. A more extensive type of maintenance is called *workover*. Using a scaled-down version of a drilling rig, a high-pressure pump forces liquids through the tubing to the bottom of the well, outside the tubing, then back to the surface. This allows the well pressure to be controlled from the surface, and work then can be performed on the well. There are companies that specialize entirely in well servicing or workover maintenance.

Hydrocarbons are removed from the ground in complex mixtures of water, oil, and natural gas and must be separated and treated at the well site. Two tanks are usually used; one will be filled while the other is being gauged for its oil content and emptied into a tank truck or pipeline.

Large pipelines carry the natural gas production from the well to market, while the water is sometimes reinjected into the field to help maintain reservoir pressure, which helps in the production of more oil.

Natural gas is becoming increasingly popular because it is one of the most environmentally friendly energy sources in use today. It is widely used for industrial purposes as well as by most consumers for cooking and heating. Therefore, large supplies are kept near market areas for long-range use. Oil and natural gas produced offshore also must be brought ashore by pipelines, which are required to be buried below the mud line in water depths fewer than two hundred feet.

Specially equipped semisubmersible barges lay lines in water depths ranging to one thousand feet, while vessels using reel-type equipment can lay lines in water depths of three thousand feet. In shallow waters with mild sea conditions, the oil is stored in tanks and transferred to barges.

How petroleum is transported from the well site to refineries and the marketplace will be detailed in Chapter 5.

Employment Opportunities

The many companies that perform the services listed above employ a variety of personnel for both in-house and fieldwork.

Professional Jobs

Students interested in any type of engineering careers should concentrate on math, English, physics, and chemistry. Other important courses are computer science, geology, mechanical drawing, economics, and government or social studies.

For professional jobs in the production field, a bachelor's, master's, or doctoral degree is required. The search for petroleum is becoming increasingly complex, requiring personnel with advanced education and experience. Many professionals such as engineers, geologists, or geophysicists are now being given management opportunities. Some are involved in the day-to-day production activities, while others hold support staff engineering positions.

Nonprofessional Jobs

For nonprofessional production jobs, vocational training and/or previous experience are usually recommended. A minimum of a high school diploma is required as new technology develops and becomes applicable. Many of these jobs also call for strength, stamina, and the ability to work outdoors in a variety of weather conditions.

An example of a job related to producing and recovering oil is that of a *pumper*, who is responsible for operating steam, gas, gasoline, electric, or diesel pumps and auxiliary equipment to restore and control flow of oil from wells. He or she will open valves to regulate flow of oil from wells to storage tanks or into pipelines and turn valves to adjust the pressure of the separator, which separates natural gas from oil. The pumper also reads flow meters, gauges oil in tanks with calibrated steel tape, and prepares reports of amount and quality of oil pumped and in storage. He or she also collects and bottles samples of the oil for laboratory analysis and lubricates and repairs pumps using a grease gun, oilcan, and hand tools.

The pumper also examines pipelines for leaks, reports major breakdowns and well difficulties, and may test and treat oil to reduce water and sediment content according to specifications for pipeline transportation of oil.

This position requires someone with excellent mechanical and problem-solving abilities. According to the *Occupational Outlook Handbook*, 2006–2007, the median hourly salary for a wellhead pumper in the United States in 2004 was $16.73.

Another related position is that of a *treater*, who operates chemical, electrical, and centrifugal oil treatment units to remove sediment and water from crude oil before it is transported by pipeline to refineries. The treater will open valves and start pumps to pump oil from storage tanks to treating units. He or she will open valves to mix specified chemicals with oil and adjust the controls to heat the mixture to a specified temperature. The treater starts the centrifugal machines that break up oil and water emulsions and drain off water, and opens valves and starts pumps to transfer oil into settling tanks, where sediment is precipitated from oil.

Other job responsibilities of a treater include testing samples in gravity- or centrifugal-separation machines to determine the content of oil specified for pipeline transportation. The treater also pumps treated oil into pipelines leading to a refinery and cleans and lubricates motors, pumps, and other moving parts of units. The treater also has to record data, such as volume of oil treated, operating temperatures of units, and test results. In some cases, a treater also may operate pumps at oil-well sites.

According to the *Occupational Outlook Handbook*, the median hourly salary for a service unit operator, oil, gas, and mining in the United States in 2004 was $15.87.

According to Service Canada, hourly wages are C$20.88 for the category of oil and gas well drilling workers, and services operators are close to the average of C$18.07. Service Canada's outlook to 2009 in this field is fair because the employment growth rate will likely be average; however, the high demand for energy products will continue and should create job openings. The retirement rate will likely be below average, and the number of retiring workers should not contribute significantly to job openings. The number of job seekers will likely match the number of job openings.

A good resource for more jobs in this field is the *Occupational Outlook Handbook* (www.bls.gov/oco) in the "oil and gas extraction" section; the *Dictionary of Occupational Titles* (www.occupational info.org), and *Career Guide to Industries* (www.bls.gov/oco/cg). More information about employment in Canada can be found at www.jobfutures.ca.

5

Getting Petroleum to Market

Transporting petroleum from the well site to the consumer is a complex process involving several methods of delivery. The transportation systems primarily used by the petroleum industry are pipelines, tankers and barges, highway tank trucks, and railroad tank cars. Each is used for a different purpose, and each is designed to move natural gas, crude oil, or its by-products in an efficient, economic, and environmentally sound manner.

Underground Pipelines

Probably the most common—and surely the least visible—means of transportation is the pipeline. Hundreds of thousands of miles of these lines crisscross the country, delivering millions of barrels of petroleum products and billions of cubic feet of natural gas to refineries, processing plants, and consumers. Three kinds of pipelines are used:

- **Gathering lines.** Usually the smallest and used to move oil from producing wells to field storage tanks
- **Crude oil trunk lines.** Used to transport oil from storage tanks to refineries
- **Product trunk lines.** Used to transport refined products to regional distribution centers

One of the best-known oil pipelines is the eight-hundred-mile Trans-Alaska Pipeline System, one of the largest privately financed construction projects in history at a cost of about $8 billion when it was completed in 1977. A longer but less costly oil pipeline is the twelve-hundred-mile All American Pipeline, built from California to the East Texas Gulf Coast in the mid-1980s.

One of the most historic pipelines is the nine-thousand-plus-mile Texas Eastern Pipeline, built through a partnership between the U.S. government and eleven petroleum companies during World War II.

Before the pipeline was built, German U-boats were sinking U.S. tankers carrying oil from the Gulf of Mexico to the northeast United States for civilian and military use—and to Europe to fight the war. In record time, the twenty-four-inch-diameter pipeline—which became known as the "Big Inch"—was built and transporting crude oil from Longview, Texas, to the Northeast. A second, twenty-inch-diameter pipeline known as the "Little Big Inch" was built alongside it to carry petroleum products to the East. Both lines have been recognized as playing a significant role in the Allies' victory.

After the war, the pipelines were placed out to bid, and newly created Texas Eastern Transmission Company was awarded the bid. The company converted the Big Inch to natural gas, and today the pipeline is owned by Spectra Energy, based in Houston, Texas. The Little Big Inch continues to carry petroleum products and is an indirect subsidiary of EPCO, Inc., also based in Houston.

Pipelines under construction on land must follow strict environmental and government regulations. For instance, pipeline builders must negotiate with each landowner where the pipeline will cross. The builder also is responsible for putting together the necessary equipment and crew needed to construct the pipeline. Pipeline construction requires hundreds of workers from the beginning to the end of the project. On some large projects, as many as two thousand workers may be needed throughout the construction phase.

Most pipelines are built underground in a trench dug deep enough to provide an adequate cover. After welders join various lengths of pipe that have been brought to the site, the line is hoisted and laid in the ditch. Dirt is used to cover the line and the area is cleaned up.

To help move oil through pipelines at about three to five miles per hour, pumping stations are established along the route. The distance between each is determined by the terrain, type of oil or product being moved through the line, and the size of the pipe. The flow of the oil is directed by a centrally located operator who controls the pump as well as monitors and controls the flow rate and pumping pressure system. Most systems are now automated and controlled by computer. Compressor stations located along a natural gas pipeline route increase the pressure on the gas to move it in transmission lines or into storage.

Products are moved through pipelines in shipments called *batches*. To separate the batches, an inflatable rubber ball is used. To clean out residue from a previous batch and to keep materials from building up, a scraper, called a *pig,* is run through the line. Some pipelines require that workers remove and clean the pig at each pumping station. It is then replaced and continues through the line.

Other maintenance performed on pipelines include leak detection, which can be observed either from an aircraft flying over the right of way or by a pipeline company employee walking along the pipeline. Regular communications about the pipeline's schedule also are considered maintenance. Companies use private telecommunications systems as well as mobile radios and cell phones. Emerging technology allows companies to integrate computers with microwave systems to improve communications. Pipeline operations are monitored around the clock from a control center to ensure they are operating properly.

Large seagoing vessels used to construct pipelines in offshore waters are called *lay barges.* One of the largest is called a *superbarge,* which can house up to 350 workers and store as much as twenty-thousand tons of pipe.

Tankers and Barges

Using waterways for transporting products is not unique to the petroleum industry. But at no time in the history of the United States were the value of oil tankers realized than during World War II. Because of tankers, along with the Big Inch and Little Big Inch pipelines, it is believed that the Allies were victorious because they were able to carry large amounts of crude produced in the West to the fighting forces in Europe.

Most of the world's petroleum is transported by tankers. A tanker of average size can carry about thirty thousand tons—as much gasoline, diesel fuel, or home-heating oil as seventeen hundred tanker trucks. America imports about 60 percent of its oil; most of it arrives by tanker. It is expected that unless the United States establishes an energy policy encouraging domestic production within the next several decades, about ten million barrels a day of crude oil and petroleum products will be delivered to the United States by tankers.

Barges are used extensively on America's thirty-five-thousand-mile inland waterway system, including lakes and rivers. This type of vessel is used to transport petroleum products between refining centers and consumers. A barge can carry between eight thousand and fifty thousand barrels of petroleum. In the United States, some barges can carry up to one hundred thousand barrels or more. Oceangoing barges can carry even larger amounts.

Tank Trucks and Rail Cars

Probably the most visible method of transporting petroleum products is by tank truck, those massive vehicles that can carry loads ranging from eight thousand to ten thousand gallons each. Most modern tank trucks are built of lighter materials, such as aluminum alloys, and run on diesel fuel, which can sometimes be more economical than gasoline on long hauls. Trucks also are used to transport such finished products as gasoline, kerosene, and jet fuel from the refineries to a customer distribution point.

Railroad tank cars are used to carry crude oil, petroleum products, and chemicals, with each capable of holding between four thousand and thirty-three thousand gallons. Most railcars are specially designed to handle certain products, depending on whether they need to be kept hot or cold. New materials also are being used to make the rail tank cars safer and more efficient.

Employment Opportunities

There are as many opportunities for employment in the transportation segment of the petroleum industry as there are methods of moving petroleum and its by-products. Truck drivers, seagoing personnel, railroad workers, and pipeline operators are all needed to transport products to their destinations. Following are a few examples of opportunities in the transportation of petroleum. Most of this information is from the *Occupational Outlook Handbook*, 2006–2007.

Pipeline Workers

Pipeline companies provide a variety of employment opportunities, including design, construction, and operations/maintenance.

Design

Pipeline drafters prepare the drawings of topographical and relief maps used in major construction or civil engineering projects such as pipelines. Employers are most interested in applicants with well-developed drafting and mechanical drawing skills; knowledge of drafting standards, mathematics, science, and engineering technology; and a solid background in CADD (computer-aided design and drafting) techniques. In addition, communication and problem-solving skills are important.

In general, employment of drafters is expected to grow more slowly than the average (0 to 8 percent) for all occupations through 2014. However, industrial growth and ever more complex design problems associated with new products and manufacturing processes will increase the demand for drafting services. Further, drafters are beginning to break out of the traditional drafting role and do work traditionally performed by engineers and architects, thus increasing demand for drafters.

Drafters' earnings vary by specialty, location, and level of responsibility. Median annual earnings of architectural and civil drafters in the United States were $39,190 in May 2004.

Construction

Pipe layers generally work a standard forty-hour week. However, those involved in maintaining pipe systems, including those who provide maintenance services under contract, may have to work evening or weekend shifts, as well as be on call. These maintenance workers may spend quite a bit of time traveling to and from work sites. Training is usually through a company or through formal apprenticeship programs.

Employment of pipe layers is expected to grow about as fast as average (9 to 17 percent) for all occupations through the year 2014. Pipe layers (including plumbers, pipe fitters, and steamfitters) are among the highest paid construction occupations. In May 2004, median hourly earnings of pipe layers in the United States were $13.68.

Operations/Maintenance

A pipe liner maintains and repairs pipelines, pumping stations, and tank farms by performing any combination of the following duties as a member of a crew: removes rust and foreign substances from meters and valves with sandblasting equipment; pours corrosion-resistant material over pipe or applies it with a brush or spray gun; wraps pipe with strips of paper or fabric to prevent corrosion and leakage; and drives and operates such equipment as backhoes, bulldozers, and side booms to dig ditches, lay pipe, and backfill ditches.

He or she positions materials, pipes, fittings, and pumping equipment for carpenters, mechanics, and welders; installs screw-pipe and manifold connections using wrenches and pipe tongs; and cleans storage tanks using squeegees and rakes.

The pipe liner, using earth-moving equipment, picks, and shovels, also dismantles and restores items such as fences, gates, and waterlines that inhibit pipeline work; cuts brushes, trees, and weeds with axes and hoes; digs drainage ditches using shovels; and gathers trash, pipe parts, and equipment to clear grounds along pipeline rights-of-way. He or she may also walk along the pipeline to detect leaks or operate pumping equipment or pipe-cleaning and wrapping machines to apply dope and wrap pipe. Salaries vary, dependent upon experience, location, and type of work. According to www.salary.com, the average salary for an entry-level pipeline technician was about $50,000.

Truck Drivers

Truck drivers deliver gasoline, fuel oil, lubricating oil, or liquefied petroleum gas to customers. The driver is responsible for positioning the truck at the filling rack, opening valves, and starting pumps to fill the tank. He or she is responsible for reading gauges or meters and recording the quantity loaded.

Persons interested in a career as a truck driver for petroleum products should have a clean driving record. Some states require workers to obtain a commercial drivers license. In general, most truck drivers may have to pass a physical and a written exam, as well as a driving test. They should have good hearing, at least 20/40 vision with or without glasses or corrective lenses, be able to lift heavy objects, and be in good health. Gasoline tank truck drivers are responsible for getting to a destination in a timely and safe manner.

Once there, the driver attaches the hoses and operates the pumps on the truck to transfer the gasoline to gas stations' storage tanks.

Job opportunities should be favorable for truck drivers, according to the *Occupational Outlook Handbook*, 2006–2007. In addition to growth in demand for truck drivers, numerous job openings will occur as experienced drivers leave this large occupation to transfer to other fields of work, retire, or leave the labor force for other reasons. Jobs vary greatly in terms of earnings, weekly work hours, the number of nights spent on the road, and quality of equipment. There may be competition for the jobs with the highest earnings and the most favorable work schedules. Median hourly earnings of heavy-truck and tractor-trailer drivers in the United States were $16.11 in May 2004.

Other Opportunities

Other jobs available in the petroleum transportation industry include dispatchers, dock supervisors, gaugers, compression-station workers, distribution workers, construction and maintenance inspectors, oil pumpers, station engineers, barrel fillers, gas-transfer operators, and loaders. Some of these offer entry-level positions as helpers or apprentices.

According to Service Canada, hourly wages are C$20.88 for the category of oil- and gas-well drilling workers and services operators. Service Canada's outlook to 2009 in this field is fair because the employment growth rate will likely be average; however, the high demand for energy products will continue and should create job openings. The retirement rate will likely be below average, and the number of retiring workers should not contribute significantly to job openings. The number of job seekers will likely match the number of job openings.

For more information about employment in the petroleum industry, refer to the *Occupational Outlook Handbook* (www.bls.gov/oco) under the "oil and gas extraction" section; the *Dictionary of Occupational Titles* (www.occupationalinfo.org), and *Career Guide to Industries* (www.bls.gov/oco/cg). For more information about employment in Canada, go to www.jobfutures.ca.

6

Refining and Marketing

Crude oil must be refined before it can be used. The plant where the oil is separated into various components and made into the hundreds of products we use each day is called a *refinery*.

The first refinery to open after the Drake discovery was built near Oil Creek in 1860 by William Barnsdall and William H. Abbott. That refinery probably looked a lot different from today's refinery, which appears to be a complex maze of pipes and storage tanks. As modern refining facilities become more and more automated, highly skilled workers are needed to operate them.

There are hundreds of refineries currently operating in the United States. Their refining capacity ranges from the smaller operations (190 barrels a day) to larger plants that process more than half a million barrels of crude oil daily.

One barrel of oil is typically refined into:

- Gasoline—19.4 gallons
- Distillate fuel oil (includes both home-heating oil and diesel fuel)—10.5 gallons
- Kerosene-type jet fuel—4.1 gallons
- Residual fuel oil (heavy oils used as fuels in industry, marine transportation, and for electric power generation)—1.7 gallons
- Liquefied refinery gases—1.5 gallons
- Still gas—1.8 gallons
- Coke—2.2 gallons
- Asphalt and road oil—1.4 gallons
- Raw material for petrochemicals—1.1 gallons
- Lubricants—0.4 gallon
- Kerosene—0.2 gallon
- Other—0.4 gallon

(Note: Figures are based on average yields for U.S. refineries in 2005. One barrel contains forty-two gallons of crude oil. The total volume of products made is 2.7 gallons greater than the original forty-two gallons of crude oil. This represents "processing gain.")

Because there are different types of crude oils, the process of refining is different for each. Some crude oils contain a large amount of paraffin wax, with little or no asphalt. This type of oil yields wax, as well as large amounts of high-grade lubricating oil. As the name implies, asphalt-base crude oil has a large amount of asphaltic materials, while mixed-base crudes have quantities of both paraffin wax and asphalt.

Contrary to popular belief, crude oil is not always a thick, black, gooey substance. Some oils are nearly colorless, while others are amber, green, or brown. Crude oil that has more than 1 percent sulfur and other mineral impurities are called *sour crudes*. Those that have less than 1 percent sulfur are called *sweet crudes*.

Refining Petroleum

All crude oils, no matter what type, must undergo three refining processes: separation, conversion, and treatment.

There are various methods used to separate the components of crude oil. The most common is the distillation process. The crude oil is heated, and as the components vaporize, they are drawn off for further processing. Other ways to separate the oil into its parts (also called *fractions*) include the use of solvents, absorption, and crystallization.

After the crude oil is separated, it must undergo a conversion process. This is where the molecular structure of the separated fractions is changed to produce specific products. This particular process began in response to a growing demand for gasoline. The conversion step lets refiners produce gasoline from groups of hydrocarbons not normally found in the gasoline range.

Processes using heat and pressure and/or chemical catalysts are used to break heavier oils into lighter ones to make such products as gasoline. Similar methods are used to combine several light molecules into a few heavy ones in order to make high-octane fuels.

In the third refining process, oil products are chemically treated to remove impurities and to improve products.

The natural gas refining business became a thriving industry with the advent of natural gas pipelines. During the conditioning processes, water, impurities, and excess hydrocarbon liquids are removed. Common plant processes include oil absorption, fractionation, dehydration, and cryogenic processing.

Manufacturing Petrochemicals

During the refining process, two of the forty-two gallons in each barrel of oil are chemicals used to manufacture other products. These chemicals, known as *petrochemicals*, are primarily composed of hydrogen, carbon, nitrogen, and sulfur. When the molecules of these ingredients are changed and shifted in various combinations, hundreds of chemical products, called *feedstocks*, are produced for use in commonly used items.

A petrochemical plant turns petroleum derivatives into feedstocks used to manufacture a wide variety of products used on a daily basis. These products include ammonia—as well as polyethylene and polypropylene—which are used to make items such as appliance and automotive parts, luggage, plastic toys, and containers. Other feedstocks are used to make diverse items such as cups and glasses, furniture, fibers to make wearing apparel, surfboards, and paints.

There are about 149 refineries now in operation in the United States. Most of them are located in what is known as this country's *Golden Crescent*, a seven-hundred-mile coastal strip between Brownsville, Texas, and New Orleans, Louisiana. This area is noted for its available water transportation, refining complexes, and oil and gas fields.

Employment Opportunities in Refining

There are a variety of careers available in the refining segment of the petroleum industry. Professional opportunities include those of *process engineers* and *chemical engineers*. Process engineers oversee refinery operations; chemical engineers work in many phases of the production of chemicals and chemical products.

Chemical Engineers

Chemical engineers apply the principles of chemistry to solve problems involving the production or use of chemicals and biochemicals. They design equipment and processes for large-scale chemical manufacturing, plan and test methods of manufacturing products and treating by-products, and supervise production. Some may specialize in a particular chemical process, such as oxidation or polymerization. Others specialize in a particular field, such as materials science, or in the development of specific products. They must be aware of all aspects of chemicals manufacturing and how the manufacturing process affects the environment and the safety of workers and consumers.

Employment

Chemical engineers in the United States held thirty-one thousand jobs in 2004, according to the *Occupational Outlook Handbook, 2006–2007*. Some branches of engineering are concentrated in particular industries and geographic areas—for example, petroleum engineering jobs tend to be located in areas with sizable petroleum deposits, such as Texas, Louisiana, Oklahoma, Alaska, and California. In Canada, most chemical engineers work in Ontario and Alberta.

Job Outlook

Chemical engineers are expected to have employment growth about as fast as the average (9 to 17 percent) for all occupations through 2014. Although overall employment in the chemical manufacturing industry is expected to decline, chemical companies will continue to research and develop new chemicals and more efficient processes to increase output of existing chemicals. Most employment growth for chemical engineers will be in service industries, such as scientific research and development services (including energy), according to the *Occupational Outlook Handbook*.

Earnings

Chemical engineers in the United States are the second-highest paid in the engineering profession, averaging $53,813 in 2005, compared to $61,516 for petroleum engineers. According to Service Canada, hourly wages in Canada are C$31.10.

Petroleum Pump System Operators, Refinery Operators, and Gaugers

Employees who work at these jobs control the operation of petroleum refining or processing units. They may specialize in controlling manifold and pumping systems, gauging or testing oil in storage tanks, or regulating the flow of oil into pipelines.

According to the *Occupational Outlook Handbook*, about forty-three thousand employees in the United States worked in this field in 2004. The projected employment outlook to 2014 is expected to decline.

A number of nonengineering jobs in the refining industry do not require a college education. Many companies provide classroom and on-the-job training. However, because modern refineries are highly automated, workers should have good mechanical aptitude and knowledge of specialized equipment.

Other jobs associated with the refining field include those in the transportation area, including truck drivers and barge, pipeline, tanker, and railroad workers. Salaries for these workers vary from company to company and depend on the amount of experience.

Marketing Petroleum

One of the most fascinating aspects of the petroleum industry is marketing, whether trading crude oil on the world market or retailing petroleum products. While the oil market has always had some flux, in recent years it has become more volatile because of the influence of worldwide political events and increased competition.

Market Research Analysts

Vertically integrated oil companies are large firms involved in all aspects of the oil industry—from exploration to retail sales of its products. Because such a company is totally involved in the entire process, marketing plans are integrated within the company's exploration, drilling, production, refining, transportation, and distribution activities.

Oil marketers, whether large or small, must determine the consumer market in order to balance supply and demand. Research must be conducted into present, near future, and distant future demand. Using the material from this research, marketers can determine how well their advertising and public relations programs are working.

Market (or *marketing)* research analysts are concerned with the potential sales of a product or service. By gathering statistical data on competitors and examining prices, sales, and methods of marketing and distribution, they analyze data on past sales to predict future sales.

Survey researchers collect information used for research, making fiscal or policy decisions, measuring the effectiveness of those decisions for improving customer satisfaction.

Working Conditions

In general, market and survey researchers generally have structured work schedules. Some often work alone, writing reports, preparing statistical charts, and using computers, but they also may be an integral part of a research team. Market researchers who conduct personal interviews have frequent contact with the public. Most work under pressure of deadlines and tight schedules, which may require overtime. Their routine may be interrupted by special requests for data, as well as by the need to attend meetings or conferences. Travel may be necessary.

Employment

Market and survey researchers in the United States held about 212,000 jobs in 2004, most of which—190,000—were held by market research analysts. Because of the applicability of market research to many industries, market research analysts are employed throughout the economy.

Training, Other Qualifications, and Advancement

A bachelor's degree is the minimum educational requirement for many market and survey research jobs. However, a master's degree may be required, especially for technical positions, and it increases opportunities for advancement to more responsible positions. Also, continuing education is important to keep current with the latest methods of developing, conducting, and analyzing surveys and other data.

Market and survey researchers may earn advanced degrees in business administration, marketing, statistics, communications, or some closely related discipline. In addition to completing courses in business, marketing, and consumer behavior, prospective market and survey researchers should take other liberal arts and social science courses, including economics, psychology, English, and sociology. Because of the importance of quantitative skills to market and survey researchers, courses in mathematics, statistics, sampling theory and survey design, and computer science are extremely helpful. Many corporation and government executives have a strong background in marketing.

While in college, aspiring market and survey researchers should gain experience gathering and analyzing data, conducting interviews or surveys, and writing reports on their findings. This experience can prove invaluable later in obtaining a full-time position in the field because much of the initial work may center on these duties. With experience, market and survey researchers eventually are assigned their own research projects.

Much of the market and survey researcher's time is spent on precise data analysis, so those considering careers in the occupation should be able to pay attention to detail. Patience and persistence are necessary qualities because these workers must spend long hours on independent study and problem solving. Also, they must work well with others; often, market and survey researchers oversee interviews of a wide variety of individuals. Communication skills are important, too, because researchers must be able to present their findings both orally and in writing in a clear, concise manner.

While certification currently is not required for market and survey researchers, the Marketing Research Association (MRA) offers a certification program for professional researchers. Certification is based on education and experience requirements, as well as on continuing education.

Job Outlook

Employment of market and survey researchers in the United States is expected to grow faster than average (18 to 26 percent) for all occupations through 2014. Many job openings are likely to result from the need to replace experienced workers who transfer to other occupations or who retire or leave the labor force for other reasons. According to Service Canada, work prospects in Canada are fair.

Job opportunities should be best for those with a master's or Ph.D. degree in marketing or a related field and strong quantitative skills. Bachelor's degree holders may face competition; many positions, especially the more technical ones, require a master's or higher degree. Among bachelor's degree holders, those with good quantitative skills, including a strong background in mathematics, statistics, survey design, and computer science, will have the best opportunities. Ph.D.s in marketing and related fields should have a range of opportunities in industry and consulting firms.

Demand for market research analysts should be strong because of an increasingly competitive economy. Marketing research provides organizations valuable feedback from purchasers, allowing companies to evaluate consumer satisfaction and plan more effectively for the future. As companies seek to expand their market and as consumers become better informed, the need for marketing professionals will increase. In addition, as globalization of the marketplace continues, market researchers will increasingly be utilized to analyze foreign markets and competition for goods and services.

Earnings

Median annual earnings of market research analysts in the United States in May 2004 were $56,140. The middle 50 percent earned between $40,510 and $79,990. The lowest 10 percent earned less than $30,890, and the highest 10 percent earned more than $105,870.

Median annual earnings of survey researchers in the United States in May 2004 were $26,490. The middle 50 percent earned between $17,920 and $41,390. The lowest 10 percent earned less than $15,330, and the highest 10 percent earned more than $56,740. Median annual earnings of survey researchers in other professional, scientific, and technical services were $22,880. Service Canada notes that hourly wages are C$26.22, and the rate of wage growth is also above average.

Sellers

Independent marketers usually sell a product or products at some point in the marketing chain. Such companies purchase name-brand refiners' overstock or products from independent refineries. These independent marketers also may be brokers—people who buy and sell primarily on paper. Often they purchase products on the spot market; that is, they buy on the spot as the immediate market demands, rather than rely on long-term plans. Independent marketers sometimes have contracts with suppliers and also may be involved in storage, transportation, and distribution.

Independent middlemen, called *jobbers*, usually enter into a contract with the owner of the terminal company to sell that product brand wholesale. The jobber also could have his or her own retail store, where he or she resells the product from the terminal. Independent service stations may buy their fuels from the company owning the terminal or from jobbers.

Advertising, Promotions, Marketing/Sales, and Public Relations Managers

The objective of any firm is to market and sell its products or services profitably, says the *Occupational Outlook Handbook*, 2006–2007. In small firms, the owner or chief executive officer might assume all advertising, promotions, marketing, public relations, and sales responsibilities. In large firms, which may offer numerous products and services nationally or even worldwide, an executive vice president directs overall advertising, promotions, marketing, sales, and public relations policies.

Advertising, promotions, marketing/sales, and public relations managers coordinate the market research, marketing strategy, sales, advertising, promotion, pricing, product development, and public relations activities.

Advertising managers oversee advertising and promotion staffs, which usually are small, except in the largest firms. The *account executive* manages the account services department, assesses the need for advertising, and, in advertising agencies, maintains the accounts of clients. The *creative services department* develops the subject matter and presentation of advertising. The *creative director* oversees the copy chief, art director, and associated staff. The *media director* oversees planning groups that select the communication media—for example, radio, television, newspapers, magazines, the Internet, or outdoor signs—to disseminate the advertising.

Promotions managers supervise staffs of promotion specialists. These managers direct promotion programs that combine advertising with purchase incentives to increase sales. In an effort to establish closer contact with purchasers—dealers, distributors, or consumers—promotion programs may use direct mail, telemarketing, television or radio advertising, catalogs, exhibits, inserts in newspapers, Internet advertisements or Web sites, in-store displays or product endorsements, and special events. Purchasing incentives may include discounts, samples, gifts, rebates, coupons, sweepstakes, and contests.

Marketing managers develop the firm's marketing strategy in detail. With the help of subordinates, including *product development managers* and *market research managers*, they estimate the demand for products and services offered by the firm and its competitors. In addition, they identify potential markets—for example, business firms, wholesalers, retailers, government, or the general public. Marketing managers develop pricing strategy to help firms maximize profits and market share while ensuring that the firm's customers are satisfied.

In collaboration with sales, product development, and other managers, they monitor trends that indicate the need for new products and services, and they oversee product development. Marketing managers work with advertising and promotion managers to promote the firm's products and services and to attract potential users.

Public relations managers direct publicity programs to a targeted audience. They use every available communication medium to maintain the support of the specific group upon which their organization's success depends, such as consumers, stockholders, or the general public. They also evaluate advertising and promotion programs for compatibility with public relations efforts and serve as the eyes and ears of top management.

Public relations managers may confer with labor relations managers to produce internal company communications—such as newsletters about employee-management relations—and with financial managers to produce company reports. They also assist company executives in drafting speeches, arranging interviews, and maintaining other forms of public contact; oversee company archives; and respond to requests for information.

Working Conditions

Advertising, promotions, marketing, public relations, and sales managers work in offices close to those of a company's top managers. Long hours, including evenings and weekends, are common.

In 2004, about two-thirds of advertising, promotions, marketing, and public relations managers worked more than forty hours a week. Working under pressure is unavoidable when schedules change and problems arise, but deadlines and goals must still be met. Substantial travel may also be involved. For example, attendance at meetings sponsored by associations or industries often is mandatory.

Sales managers travel to national, regional, and local offices and to the offices of various dealers and distributors. Advertising and promotions managers may travel to meet with clients or representatives of communications media. At times, public relations managers travel to meet with special-interest groups or government officials. Job transfers between headquarters and regional offices are common, particularly among sales managers.

Employment

Advertising, promotions, marketing, public relations, and sales managers in the United States held about 646,000 jobs in 2004. These managers were found in virtually every industry. Marketing managers held more than one-fourth of the jobs; the professional, scientific, and technical services industries employed almost one-third of marketing managers. About one-fourth of advertising and promotions managers worked in the professional, scientific, and technical services industries, as well as the information industries, including advertising and related services and publishing industries.

Training, Other Qualifications, and Advancement

A wide range of educational backgrounds is suitable for entry into advertising, promotions, marketing, public relations, and sales managerial jobs, but many employers prefer those with experience in related occupations plus a broad liberal arts background. A bachelor's degree in sociology, psychology, literature, journalism, or philosophy, among other subjects, is acceptable. However, requirements vary, depending upon the particular job.

For marketing, sales, and promotions management positions, some employers prefer a bachelor's or master's degree in business administration with an emphasis in marketing. Courses in business law, economics, accounting, finance, mathematics, and statistics are advantageous. For advertising management positions, some employers prefer a bachelor's degree in advertising or journalism. A course of study should include marketing, consumer behavior, market research, sales, communication methods and technology, and visual arts—for example, art history and photography.

For public relations management positions, some employers prefer a bachelor's or master's degree in public relations or journalism. The applicant's curriculum should include courses in advertising, business administration, public affairs, public speaking, political science, and creative and technical writing.

For these specialties, courses in management and completing an internship while the candidate is in school are highly recommended. Familiarity with database applications is important for many positions. Computer skills are vital because marketing, product promotion, and advertising on the Internet are common. Also, the ability to communicate in a foreign language may open up employment opportunities in many rapidly growing areas around the country, especially cities with large Spanish-speaking populations.

Some associations offer certification programs for these managers. Certification—which is considered an indication of competence and achievement—is particularly important in a competitive job market. While relatively few advertising, promotions, marketing, public relations, and sales managers currently are certified, the number of managers who seek certification is expected to grow. Today, there are numerous management certification programs based on education and job performance. In addition, the Public Relations Society of America offers a certification program for public relations practitioners based on years of experience and performance on an examination.

Persons who are interested in becoming advertising, promotions, marketing, public relations, and sales managers should be mature, creative, highly motivated, resistant to stress, flexible, and decisive. The ability to communicate persuasively, both orally and in writing, with other managers, staff, and the public is vital. These managers also need tact, good judgment, and exceptional ability to establish and maintain effective personal relationships with supervisory and professional staff members and client firms.

Because of the importance and high visibility of their jobs, advertising, promotions, marketing, public relations, and sales managers often are prime candidates for advancement to the highest ranks. Well-trained, experienced, and successful managers may be promoted to higher positions in their own or another firm; some become top executives. Managers with extensive experience and sufficient capital may open their own businesses.

Job Outlook

Advertising, promotions, marketing, public relations, and sales manager jobs are highly coveted and will be sought by other managers or highly experienced professionals, resulting in keen competition. College graduates with related experience, a high level of creativity, and strong communication skills should have the best job opportunities. In particular, employers will seek those who have the computer skills to conduct advertising, promotions, marketing, public relations, and sales activities on the Internet.

Employment of advertising, promotions, marketing, public relations, and sales managers is expected to increase faster than the average (18 to 26 percent) for all occupations through 2014, spurred by intense domestic and global competition in products and services offered to consumers. However, projected employment growth varies by industry. For example, employment is projected to grow much faster than average (27 percent or more) in scientific, professional, and related services, such as computer systems design and related services, and in advertising and related services, as businesses increasingly hire contractors for these services instead of additional full-time staff. By contrast, a decline in employment is expected in many manufacturing industries.

Earnings

Median annual earnings in May 2004 for U.S. practitioners were $63,610 for advertising and promotions managers, $87,640 for marketing managers, $84,220 for sales managers, and $70,000 for public relations managers. Median annual earnings of advertising and promotions managers in May 2004 in the advertising and related services industry were $89,570. According to a National Association of Colleges and Employers survey, starting salaries for marketing majors graduating in 2005 averaged $33,873; starting salaries for advertising majors averaged $31,340.

For sales, marketing, and advertising managers, Service Canada notes that hourly wages are C$29.97, and the rate of wage growth is below average. For professional occupations in public relations and communications, the hourly wages are C$22.51, and the rate of wage growth is above average.

Other Opportunities in Marketing

There is a variety of opportunities available for persons interested in a petroleum marketing career. Administration and management positions are open to persons who have college degrees in related fields, such as business administration or marketing.

In the sales department of a major oil company, sales personnel call on retailers, wholesalers, and commercial, industrial, and agricultural customers to sell the company's products. Persons who exhibit an expertise for directing sales operations do well in managerial sales positions.

In an integrated company, technical support personnel are needed and usually require an engineering degree. Other support staff includes clerical workers, customer service representatives, accountants, attorneys, statisticians, data processing specialists, and public relations personnel. Some jobs require advanced training or education, while others offer on-the-job training.

7

Related Petroleum Occupations

The preceding chapters have covered primary careers in the petroleum industry and touched on some of the most important support service jobs needed to explore, drill, refine, and market refined products. Because the petroleum industry is so complex and covers such a broad area, thousands of workers throughout the world are needed in every aspect of the business.

Environmental Concerns

Global warming and climate change were dominating the environmental debate as this book was being written in 2007. However, it's important to remember that despite its image, the petroleum industry has continually sought new ways to retrieve petroleum that are more efficient, economical, and environmentally friendly. Ongoing research and development are key to finding ways to protect the environment from oil spills, dust, noise, and refinery emissions.

According to a survey conducted by the American Petroleum Institute (API), the U.S. oil and natural gas industry in 2004 spent $10.3 billion to protect the nation's environment—an increase of about 2.4 percent over 2003 expenditures. API estimates that the industry has spent about $88 billion to protect the environment since 1995. More than half of the $88 billion was spent in the refining sector.

Therefore, jobs working in the environmental sector are anticipated to grow substantially in the upcoming years. The information in this chapter is from the *Occupational Outlook Handbook*, 2006–2007.

Environmental Scientists

Environmental scientists use their knowledge of the physical makeup and history of the earth to protect the environment and offer environmental site assessments and advice on indoor-air quality and hazardous-waste site remediation.

Environmental scientists conduct research to identify and abate or eliminate sources of pollutants or hazards that affect people, wildlife, and their environments. Understanding the issues involved in protecting the environment—degradation, conservation, recycling, and replenishment—is central to the work of environmental scientists, who often use their skills and knowledge to design and monitor waste-disposal sites, preserve water supplies, and reclaim contaminated land and water to comply with federal environmental regulations.

Many environmental scientists do work and have training that is similar to other physical or life scientists but is applied to environmental areas. Many specialize in some specific area, such as environmental ecology and conservation, environmental chemistry, environmental biology, or fisheries science. Most environmental scientists are further classified by the specific activity they perform, although recent advances in the understanding of basic life processes within the ecosystem have blurred some traditional classifications.

Working Conditions

Most entry-level environmental scientists spend the majority of their time in the field, while more experienced workers generally devote more of their time to office or laboratory work. Some take field trips that involve physical activity. Environmental scientists in the field may work in warm or cold climates and in all kinds of weather. In their research, they may dig or chip with a hammer, scoop with a net, come in contact with water, and carry equipment in a backpack. Those in laboratories may conduct tests, run experiments, record results, and compile data.

Training, Other Qualifications, and Advancement

A bachelor's degree is adequate for a few entry-level positions, but environmental scientists increasingly need a master's degree in a natural science. A master's degree also is the minimum educational requirement for most entry-level applied research positions in private industry.

Many environmental scientists earn degrees in life science, chemistry, geology, geophysics, atmospheric science, or physics and then, either through further education or through their research interests and work experience, apply their education to environmental areas. Others earn a degree in environmental science. A bachelor's degree in environmental science offers an interdisciplinary approach to the natural sciences, with an emphasis on biology, chemistry, and geology. In addition, undergraduate environmental science majors should focus on data analysis and physical geography, particularly if they are interested in studying pollution abatement, water resources, or ecosystem protection, restoration, or management.

Understanding the geochemistry of inorganic compounds is becoming increasingly important in developing remediation goals. Those students interested in working in the environmental or regulatory fields should take courses in hydrology, hazardous-waste management, environmental legislation, chemistry, fluid mechanics, and geologic logging. An understanding of environmental regulations and government permit issues also is valuable for those planning to work in mining and oil and gas extraction.

For environmental scientists who enter the field of consulting, courses in business, finance, marketing, or economics may be useful. In addition, combining environmental science training with other disciplines such as engineering, or a technical degree coupled with a master's degree in business administration, qualifies these scientists for the widest range of jobs. They also should have some knowledge of the potential liabilities associated with some environmental work.

Students who have some experience with computer modeling, data analysis and integration, digital mapping, remote sensing, and geographic information systems will be the most prepared to enter the job market. Knowledge of the Geographic Information System (GIS) and Global Positioning System (GPS) is vital.

Environmental scientists must have excellent interpersonal skills because they usually work as part of a team with other scientists, engineers, and technicians. Strong oral and written communication skills also are essential, because writing technical reports and research proposals and communicating technical and research results to company managers, regulators, and the public are important aspects of the work. Those involved in fieldwork must have physical stamina.

Environmental scientists often begin their careers in field exploration or, occasionally, as research assistants or technicians in laboratories or offices. They are given more difficult assignments as they gain experience. Eventually, they may be promoted to project leader, program manager, or some other management and research position.

Because international work is becoming increasingly pervasive, knowledge of a second language is a valuable skill to employers.

Job Outlook

Employment of environmental scientists in the United States is expected to grow about as fast as the average for all occupations through 2014. Job growth for environmental scientists should be strongest at private-sector consulting firms. Demand will be driven largely by public policy, which will oblige companies and organizations to comply with complex environmental laws and regulations.

Job opportunities also will be spurred by a continued general awareness regarding the need to monitor the quality of the environment, to interpret the impact of human actions on terrestrial and aquatic ecosystems, and to develop strategies for restoring ecosystems.

Many environmental scientists work for consulting firms as advisers to help businesses and government comply with new regulations on issues related to underground tanks, land disposal areas, and other hazardous-waste-management facilities.

Currently, environmental consulting is maturing and evolving from investigations to remediation and engineering solutions. At the same time, the regulatory climate is evolving from a rigid structure to a more flexible risk-based approach. These factors, coupled with new federal and state initiatives that integrate environmental activities into the business process itself, will result in a greater focus on waste minimization, resource recovery, pollution prevention, and the consideration of environmental effects during product development. This shift in focus from reactive solutions to preventive management will provide many new opportunities for environmental scientists in consulting roles.

There is no similar job classification called *environmental scientist* in Canada, so it is difficult to assess the employment outlook. Those interested in further research in the environmental field can review the information under the category "environmental and conservation technologists" on the www.jobfutures.ca website.

Earnings

Median annual earnings of environmental scientists in the United States were $51,080 in May 2004. The middle 50 percent earned between $39,100 and $67,360. The lowest 10 percent earned less than $31,610, and the highest 10 percent earned more than $85,940.

According to the National Association of Colleges and Employers, beginning salary offers in July 2005 for graduates with bachelor's degrees in an environmental science averaged $31,366 a year.

For comparison, Service Canada notes that the median annual earnings for employees under the "environmental and conservation technologists" category was C$33,300. The highest salary paid was C$42,000 and the lowest was C$23,100.

Chemists

Chemists and materials scientists search for and use new knowledge about chemicals. Chemical research has led to the discovery and development of new and improved synthetic fibers, paints, adhesives, drugs, cosmetics, electronic components, lubricants, and thousands of other products. They also develop processes such as improved oil refining and petrochemical processing that save energy and reduce pollution.

Materials scientists study the structures and chemical properties of various materials to develop new products or enhance existing ones. They also determine ways to strengthen or combine materials or develop new materials for use in a variety of products. Materials science encompasses the natural and synthetic materials used in a wide range of products and structures, from airplanes, cars, and bridges to clothing and household goods.

Many chemists and materials scientists work in research and development (R&D). In basic research, they investigate properties, composition, and structure of matter and the laws that govern the combination of elements and reactions of substances. In applied R&D, they create new products and processes or improve existing ones, often using knowledge gained from basic research. For example, synthetic rubber and plastics resulted from research on small molecules uniting to form large ones, a process called *polymerization*. R&D chemists and materials scientists use computers and a wide variety of sophisticated laboratory instrumentation for modeling and simulation in their work.

The use of computers to analyze complex data has allowed chemists and materials scientists to practice combinatorial chemistry. This technique makes and tests large quantities of chemical compounds simultaneously to find those with certain desired properties. Combinatorial chemistry has allowed chemists to produce thousands of compounds more quickly and inexpensively than was formerly possible.

Chemists also work in production and quality control in chemical manufacturing plants. They prepare instructions for plant workers that specify ingredients, mixing times, and temperatures for each stage in the process. They also monitor automated processes to ensure proper product yield and test samples of raw materials or finished products to ensure that they meet industry and government standards, including regulations governing pollution. Chemists report and document test results and analyze those results in the hope of improving existing theories or developing new test methods.

Analytical chemists determine the structure, composition, and nature of substances by examining and identifying their various elements or compounds. *Organic chemists* study the chemistry of the vast number of carbon compounds that make up all living things. Organic chemists who synthesize elements or simple compounds to create new compounds or substances that have different properties and applications have developed many commercial products, such as drugs, plastics, and elastomers (elastic substances similar to rubber). *Inorganic chemists* study compounds consisting mainly of elements other than carbon, such as those in electronic components.

Physical chemists and *theoretical chemists* study the physical characteristics of atoms and molecules and the theoretical properties of matter and investigate how chemical reactions work. Their research may result in new and better energy sources. *Macromolecular chemists* study the behavior of atoms and molecules. *Materials chemists* study and develop new materials to improve existing products or make new ones.

Working Conditions

Chemists and materials scientists usually work regular hours in offices and laboratories. R&D chemists and materials scientists spend much time in laboratories but also work in offices when they do theoretical research or plan, record, and report on their lab research. Although some laboratories are small, others are large enough to incorporate prototype chemical manufacturing facilities as well as advanced equipment for chemists.

In addition to working in a laboratory, materials scientists also work with engineers and processing specialists in industrial manufacturing facilities. Chemists do some of their work in a chemical plant or outdoors—while gathering water samples to test for pollutants, for example. Some chemists are exposed to health or safety hazards when handling certain chemicals, but there is little risk if proper procedures are followed.

Training, Other Qualifications, and Advancement

A bachelor's degree in chemistry or a related discipline usually is the minimum educational requirement for entry-level chemist jobs. However, many research jobs require a master's degree or, more often, a Ph.D. While some materials scientists hold a degree in materials science, a bachelor's degree in chemistry, physics, or electrical engineering also is accepted. Many R&D jobs require a Ph.D. in materials science or a related science.

Many colleges and universities offer degree programs in chemistry. In 2005, the American Chemical Society (ACS) approved 631 bachelor's, 308 master's, and 192 doctoral degree programs. In addition to these schools, several hundred colleges and universities also offer advanced degree programs in chemistry.

Students planning careers as chemists and materials scientists should take courses in science and mathematics, should like working with their hands building scientific apparatuses and performing laboratory experiments, and should like computer modeling. Perseverance, curiosity, and the ability to concentrate on detail and to work independently are essential. Interaction among specialists in this field is increasing, especially for specialty chemists in drug development.

In addition to required courses in analytical, inorganic, organic, and physical chemistry, undergraduate chemistry majors usually study biological sciences, mathematics, physics, and increasingly, computer science. Computer courses are essential to performing modeling and simulation tasks and operating computerized laboratory equipment. This is increasingly important as combinatorial chemistry and high-throughput screening (HTS)—the ability to enhance processing capacity—techniques are more widely applied.

Those interested in the environmental field also should take courses in environmental studies and become familiar with current legislation and regulations. Specific courses should include atmospheric chemistry, water chemistry, soil chemistry, and energy. Courses in statistics are useful because both chemists and materials scientists need the ability to apply basic statistical techniques.

Because R&D chemists and materials scientists are increasingly expected to work on interdisciplinary teams, some understanding of other disciplines, including business and marketing or economics, is desirable, along with leadership ability and good oral and written communication skills. Experience, either in academic laboratories or through internships, fellowships, or work-study programs in industry, also is useful. Some employers of research chemists prefer to hire individuals with several years of postdoctoral experience.

Graduate students typically specialize in a subfield of chemistry, such as analytical chemistry or polymer chemistry, depending on their interests and the kind of work they wish to do. However, students normally need not specialize at the undergraduate level. In fact, undergraduates who are broadly trained have more flexibility when job hunting or changing jobs than if they have narrowly defined their interests. Most employers provide new graduates additional training or education.

Beginning chemists with a bachelor's degree work in quality control, perform analytical testing, or assist senior chemists in R&D laboratories. Many employers prefer chemists and materials scientists with a Ph.D., or at least a master's degree, to lead basic and applied research. Within materials science, a broad background in various sciences is preferred. This broad base may be obtained through degrees in physics, engineering, or chemistry. While many companies prefer hiring Ph.D.s, some may employ materials scientists who have bachelor's and master's degrees.

Job Outlook

Employment of chemists in the United States is expected to grow more slowly than the average (0 to 8 percent) for all occupations through 2014. Employment in the nonpharmaceutical segments of the chemical industry, a major employer of chemists, is expected to decline over the projection period.

Consequently, new chemists at all levels may experience competition for jobs in these segments, including basic chemical manufacturing and synthetic materials. In addition, those with bachelor's degrees are increasingly finding assistant research positions at smaller research organizations. Those with an advanced degree will continue to fill most senior research and upper management positions, although applicants are likely to experience competition for these jobs.

Employment in the remaining segments of the chemical industry is expected to decline as companies downsize. To control costs, most chemical companies will increasingly turn to scientific R&D services firms to perform specialized research and other work formerly done by in-house chemists. As a result, these firms will experience healthy growth. Despite downsizing, some job openings will result from the need to replace chemists who retire or otherwise leave the labor force, although not all positions will be filled. Quality control will continue to be an important issue in chemical manufacturing and other industries that use chemicals in their manufacturing processes.

Chemists also will be needed to develop and improve the technologies and processes used to produce chemicals for all purposes and to monitor and measure air and water pollutants to ensure compliance with local, state, and federal environmental regulations. Environmental research will offer many new opportunities for chemists and materials scientists.

In order to satisfy public concerns and to comply with government regulations, the chemical industry must continue to invest billions of dollars each year in new technologies that reduce pollution and clean up existing waste sites. Chemists also are needed to find ways to use less energy and to discover alternative sources of energy.

During periods of economic recession, layoffs of chemists may occur—especially in the industrial chemicals industry. The traditional chemical industry, however, provides many raw materials to the auto manufacturing and construction industries, both of which are vulnerable to temporary slowdowns during recessions.

Earnings

Median annual earnings of chemists in the United States in May 2004 were $56,060. The middle 50 percent earned between $41,900 and $76,080. The lowest 10 percent earned less than $33,170, and the highest 10 percent earned more than $98,010. Median annual earnings of materials scientists in May 2004 were $72,390. The middle 50 percent earned between $53,350 and $92,340. The lowest 10 percent earned less than $40,030, and the highest 10 percent earned more than $113,460.

According to Service Canada, the hourly wages for chemists in Canada are C$29.23, and the rate of wage growth is close to the average.

Chemical Manufacturers

Vital to industries such as construction, motor vehicles, paper, electronics, transportation, agriculture, and pharmaceuticals, chemicals are an essential component of manufacturing. Although some chemical manufacturers produce and sell consumer products such as soap, bleach, and cosmetics, most chemical products are used as intermediate products for other goods.

The basic chemicals segment produces various petrochemicals, gases, dyes, and pigments. Petrochemicals contain carbon and hydrogen and are made primarily from petroleum and natural gas. The production of both organic and inorganic chemicals occurs in this segment. Organic chemicals are used to make a wide range of products, such as dyes, plastics, and pharmaceutical products; however, the majority of these chemicals are used in the production of other chemicals. Industrial inorganic chemicals usually are made from salts, metal compounds, other minerals, and the atmosphere.

The diversity of products produced by the chemical industry also is reflected in its component establishments. For example, firms producing synthetic materials operated relatively large plants in 2004. This segment had 10 percent of reporting establishments in the chemical manufacturing industry, yet it had 18 percent of all jobs in the industry. By contrast, manufacturers of paints, coatings, and adhesive products had a greater number of establishments, each employing a much smaller number of workers. This segment made up 13 percent of the establishments in the chemical industry, yet it employed only 11 percent of all workers.

Chemical plants are located near the petroleum and natural-gas production centers along the Gulf Coast in Texas and Louisiana. Because chemical production processes often use water and chemicals are primarily exported by ship all over the world, major industrial ports are another common location of chemical plants. California, Illinois, New Jersey, New York, Ohio, Pennsylvania, South Carolina, Tennessee, and Texas had about 50 percent of the establishments in the industry in 2004. Canada's chemical industry is concentrated in three provinces: Ontario, Quebec, and Alberta.

Working Conditions

Manufacturing chemicals usually is a continuous process; this means that once a process has begun, it cannot be stopped when it is time for workers to go home. Split, weekend, and night shifts are common, and workers on such schedules usually are compensated with higher rates of pay.

Most jobs in chemical manufacturing are in large establishments. The largest 20 percent of establishments that employed fifty or more workers in 2004 had 80 percent of the industry's jobs. The plants usually are clean, although the continually running machines sometimes are loud, and the interior of many plants can be hot. Hard hats and safety goggles are mandatory and worn throughout the plant.

Hazards in the chemical industry can be substantial, but they generally are avoided through strict safety procedures. Workers are required to have protective gear and extensive knowledge of the dangers associated with the chemicals being handled. Body suits with breathing devices designed to filter out any harmful fumes are mandatory for work in dangerous environments.

In spite of the hazards associated with working with chemicals, extensive worker training in handling hazardous chemicals and chemical company safety measures have resulted in injury and illness rates for some segments of the chemical industry that are much lower than the average for the manufacturing sector.

Employment

There are many different kinds of occupations to be found in chemical manufacturing. They are primarily in the areas of production and research and development.

Production

Workers in production occupations operate and fix plant machinery, transport raw materials, and in general monitor the production process. Improvements in technology gradually are increasing the level of plant automation, reducing the number of jobs in production occupations.

Chemical plant and system operators monitor the entire production process. From chemical ingredient ratios to chemical reaction rates, the operator is responsible for the efficient operation of the chemical plant. Chemical plant operators generally advance to these positions after having acquired extensive experience and technical training in chemical production processes.

Industrial machinery mechanics and *machinery maintenance workers* repair equipment, install machines, or practice preventive maintenance in the plant. Workers advance to these jobs through apprenticeships, through formal vocational training, or by completing in-house training courses.

Inspectors, *testers*, *sorters*, *samplers*, and *weighers* ensure that the production process runs efficiently and that products meet quality standards. They refer problems to plant operators or managers.

Transportation and *material moving workers* use industrial trucks to move materials around the plant or to deliver finished products to customers. For these jobs, employers seek experienced workers with knowledge of chemical hazards, safety procedures, and regulations governing the transport of hazardous chemicals.

Research and Development

Most workers in research and development have at least a college degree, and many have advanced degrees.

As mentioned above, chemists and materials scientists carry out research over a wide range of activities, including analyzing materials, preparing new materials or modifying existing ones, studying process chemistry pathways for new or existing products, and formulating cosmetics, household care products, or paints and coatings. *Chemical engineers* design equipment and develop processes for manufacturing chemicals on a large scale. They conduct experiments to learn how processes behave and to discover new chemical products and processes. A bachelor's degree is essential for all of these jobs, and a master's degree may be preferred or required for some.

Engineering technicians and *science technicians* assist chemists and engineers in research activities and may conduct some research independently. Those with bachelor's degrees in chemistry or graduates of two-year technical institutes usually fill these positions. Some graduates of engineering programs start as technicians until an opportunity to advance into an engineering position becomes available.

Job Outlook

Although output is expected to grow, wage and salary employment in the chemical manufacturing industry in the United States, excluding pharmaceuticals and medicine, is projected to decline by 14 percent over the 2004–2014 period, compared with 14 percent growth projected for the entire economy. The expected decline in employment can be attributed to trends affecting the United States and global economies.

A number of factors will influence chemical industry employment, such as more efficient production processes, increased plant automation, the state of the national and world economy, company mergers and consolidation, increased foreign competition, the shifting of production activities to foreign countries, and environmental health and safety concerns and legislation.

Another trend in the chemical industry is the rising demand for specialty chemicals. Chemical companies are finding that to remain competitive, they must differentiate their products and produce specialty chemicals, such as advanced polymers and plastics designed for customer-specific uses—for example, a durable body panel on an automobile.

Improvements in production technology have reduced the need for workers in production; installation, maintenance, and repair;

and material moving occupations, which account for large proportions of jobs in the chemical industry. Both the application of computerized controls in standard production and the growing manufacture of specialty chemicals requiring precise, computer-controlled production methods will reduce the need for workers to monitor or directly operate equipment.

Although production facilities will be easier to run with the increased use of computers, the new production methods will require workers with a better understanding of the systems.

Foreign competition has been intensifying in most industries, and the chemical industry is no exception. Globalization—the increase in international trade and rapidly expanding foreign production capabilities—should intensify competition.

Pressure to reduce costs and streamline production is expected to result in mergers and consolidations of companies both in the United States and abroad. Mergers and consolidations are allowing chemical companies to increase profits by eliminating duplicate tasks and departments and shifting operations to locations where costs are low. U.S. companies are expected to move some production activities to developing countries—East Asia and Latin America, for example—to take advantage of rapidly expanding markets.

The chemical industry invests billions of dollars yearly in technology to reduce pollution and clean up waste sites. Concerns about waste remediation and hazardous chemicals and their effects on the environment may spur producers to create chemicals with fewer or less dangerous by-products or with by-products that can be recycled or disposed of cleanly.

The factors influencing employment in the chemical manufacturing industry will affect different segments of the industry to varying degrees. Only one segment—cleaning preparations, including soap, cleaning compounds, and toilet preparations—is projected to grow, with an increase of about 5,600 jobs. Three segments—other chemical products, basic chemical manufacturing, and synthetic materials—are projected to lose jobs: about 11,000, 46,000, and 23,000, respectively.

There is no single source to compare data for chemical manufacturing opportunities in Canada, but interested students can learn more at the Service Canada website at www.jobfutures.ca.

Earnings

Earnings in the chemical industry are higher than average. Weekly earnings for all production workers in chemical manufacturing in the United States averaged $820 in May 2004, compared with $659 in all manufacturing industries and $529 throughout private industry. The higher earnings were due, in part, to the chemical industry's practice of assigning more overtime and weekend work, which commands higher hourly rates. Wages of workers in the chemical industry vary according to occupation, the specific industry segment, and the size of the production plant.

The principal unions representing chemical workers are the International Chemical Workers Union and the Paper, Allied-Industrial, Chemical, and Energy (PACE) Workers International Union. In 2004, 12 percent of chemical manufacturing workers were union members or were covered by union contracts, compared with 14 percent of all workers.

Science Technicians

Science technicians use the principles and theories of science and mathematics to solve problems in research and development and to help invent and improve products and processes. However, their jobs are more practically oriented than those of scientists. Technicians set up, operate, and maintain laboratory instruments, monitor experiments, make observations, calculate and record results, and often develop conclusions. They must keep detailed logs of all of their work-related activities. Those who perform production work monitor manufacturing processes and may be involved in ensuring quality by testing products for proper proportions of ingredients, for purity, or for strength and durability.

As laboratory instrumentation and procedures have become more complex, the role of science technicians in research and development has expanded. In addition to performing routine tasks, many technicians now develop and adapt laboratory procedures to achieve the best results, interpret data, and devise solutions to problems, under the direction of scientists. Most science technicians specialize, learning skills and working in the same disciplines in which scientists work. Occupational titles, therefore, tend to follow the same structure as those for scientists.

Chemical technicians work with chemists and chemical engineers, developing and using chemicals and related products and equipment. Many research and development chemical technicians conduct a variety of laboratory procedures, from routine process control to complex research projects. For example, they may collect and analyze samples of air and water to monitor pollution levels, or they may produce compounds through complex organic synthesis.

Geological technicians and *petroleum technicians* measure and record physical and geologic conditions in oil or gas wells, using advanced instruments lowered into the wells or analyzing the mud from the wells. In oil and gas exploration, these technicians collect and examine geological data or use scanning electron microscopes to test geological samples to determine their petroleum content and their mineral and element composition.

Some petroleum technicians, called *scouts*, collect information about oil and gas well-drilling operations, geological and geophysical prospecting, and land or lease contracts.

Working Conditions

Science technicians work under a wide variety of conditions. Most work indoors, usually in laboratories, and have regular hours. Some occasionally work irregular hours to monitor experiments that cannot be completed during regular working hours.

Production technicians often work in eight-hour shifts around the clock. Others, such as geological and petroleum technicians, perform much of their work outdoors, sometimes in very remote locations.

Some science technicians may be exposed to hazards from equipment, chemicals, or toxic materials. Chemical technicians sometimes work with toxic chemicals or radioactive isotopes. However, these working conditions pose little risk if proper safety procedures are followed.

Employment

Science technicians in the United States held approximately 324,000 jobs in 2004, with chemical and biological technicians accounting for 39 percent of all jobs. About 23 percent of all geological and petroleum technicians worked for oil and gas extraction companies.

Chemical technicians held jobs in a wide range of manufacturing and service-providing industries. About 35 percent worked in chemical manufacturing and another 26 percent worked in professional, scientific, or technical services firms. Significant numbers of environmental science and protection technicians also worked for state and local governments and professional, scientific, and technical services firms.

Training, Other Qualifications, and Advancement

There are several ways to qualify for a job as a science technician. Many employers prefer applicants who have at least two years of specialized training or an associate's degree in applied science or science-related technology. However, because employers' preferences vary, some science technicians have a bachelor's degree in chemistry, biology, or forensic science or have taken several science and math courses at four-year colleges.

Many technical and community colleges offer associate's degrees in a specific technology or a more general education in science and mathematics. A number of two-year associate's degree programs are designed to provide easy transfer to a four-year college or university. Technical institutes usually offer technician training, but they provide less theory and general education than do technical or community colleges. The length of programs at technical institutes varies, although one-year certificate programs and two-year associate's degree programs are common.

Most chemical process technicians have a two-year degree, usually an associate's degree in process technology, although in some cases a high school diploma is sufficient. These workers usually receive additional on-the-job training. Entry-level workers whose college training encompasses extensive hands-on experience with a variety of diagnostic laboratory equipment generally require less on-the-job training. Those with a high school diploma typically begin work as trainees under the direct supervision of a more experienced process technician. Many with only a high school diploma eventually earn a two-year degree in process technology, which is often paid for by their employer.

Persons interested in careers as science technicians should take as many high school science and math courses as possible. Science courses taken beyond high school, in an associate's or bachelor's degree program, should be laboratory oriented, with an emphasis on bench skills. A solid background in applied basic chemistry, physics, and math is vital. Because computers often are used in research and development laboratories, technicians should have strong computer skills, especially in computer modeling.

Communication skills also are important: technicians often are required to report their findings both orally and in writing. In addition, technicians should be able to work well with others, because teamwork is common. Organizational ability, an eye for detail, and skill in interpreting scientific results are important as well. A high mechanical aptitude, attention to detail, and analytical thinking are all important characteristics of science technicians.

Technicians usually begin work as trainees in routine positions under the direct supervision of a scientist or a more experienced technician. Job candidates whose training or educational background encompasses extensive hands-on experience with a variety of laboratory equipment, including computers and related equipment, usually require a short period of on-the-job training.

As they gain experience, technicians take on more responsibility and carry out assignments under only general supervision, and some eventually become supervisors. However, technicians employed at universities often have their fortunes tied to those of particular professors; when those professors retire or leave, these technicians face uncertain employment prospects.

Job Outlook

Job opportunities in the United States are expected to be best for graduates of applied science technology programs who are well trained on equipment used in industrial and government laboratories and production facilities. As the instrumentation and techniques used in industrial research, development, and production become increasingly more complex, employers are seeking individuals with highly developed technical and communication skills.

Overall employment of science technicians is expected to increase about as fast as the average (9 to 17 percent) for all occupations through the year 2014. Job growth for chemical technicians is projected to be slower than average (0 to 8 percent). The chemical manufacturing industry, the major employer of chemical technicians, is anticipated to experience a decline in overall employment as companies downsize and turn to outside contractors to provide specialized services.

Employment of environmental science and protection technicians should grow about as fast as the average. These workers will be needed to help regulate waste products; collect air, water, and soil samples for measuring levels of pollutants; monitor compliance with environmental regulations; and clean up contaminated sites.

Slower-than-average (somewhere between 0 and 8 percent) employment growth is expected for geological and petroleum technicians because employment in the oil and gas extraction and mining industries, which are among the largest employers of geological and petroleum technicians, is expected to decline. Due to a lack of qualified candidates, prospective job seekers should experience little competition for positions, especially in energy-related fields.

Job opportunities also will be favorable in professional, scientific, and technical services firms because geological and petroleum technicians will be needed to assist environmental scientists and geoscientists as they provide consultation services for companies regarding environmental policy and federal government mandates, such as those requiring lower sulfur emissions.

Along with opportunities created by growth, many job openings should arise from the need to replace technicians who retire or leave the labor force for other reasons. During periods of economic recession, science technicians may be laid off.

Service Canada predicts that the outlook for chemical technologists and technicians is fair. Job opportunities will depend primarily on the prosperity of rubber, plastics, and chemical products industries, which are, in turn, strongly affected by the ups and downs of foreign markets.

Earnings

Median hourly earnings of science technicians in the United States in May 2004 were: geological and petroleum technicians, $19.35; chemical technicians, $18.35; and environmental science and protection technicians, including health, $16.99.

In 2005, the average annual salary in nonsupervisory, supervisory, and managerial positions in the federal government was $62,854 for geodetic technicians.

According to Service Canada, workers classified as chemical technologists and technicians earned hourly wages of approximately C$21.05.

Miscellaneous Employment

Aside from very specific needs, the petroleum industry also needs employees who are well trained in computers, business, and other career areas. Following are a few that are also critical to the petroleum industry.

Computer Systems

Energy firms have taken advantage of technical advances made in computer software to make their operations more efficient. Major oil companies need computer specialists in a variety of business areas; exploration, production, and process; administration; operations; voice and data communications; and technology.

Business

As in any other major industry, the petroleum field requires a vast number of business professionals. Employees with a finance background work with a company's comptroller and deal with cash, asset and liability management, as well as financial planning, forecasting, and economic analysis. They also may be involved in structuring the financing of large capital projects, a common occurrence in the petroleum business. As part of the finance team at a large petroleum company, a worker will probably have to interface with bank representatives, as well as other professionals from companies that may be participating in a joint venture.

Accounting professionals in a petroleum company are responsible for preparing financial statements and reports, conducting audits, and maintaining internal financial controls. As a result of accounting scandals at several large corporate companies, the United States Congress in 2002 passed legislation in an effort to curb corporate accounting fraud. This legislation—called Sarbanes-Oxley for the bill's congressional sponsors and better known as SOX—requires public companies to maintain well-functioning internal controls to ensure the accuracy and reliability of their financial reporting. It also holds the company's chief executive personally responsible for falsely reporting financial information.

These changes have led to increased scrutiny of company finances and accounting procedures and should create opportunities for accountants and auditors, particularly CPAs, to audit financial records more thoroughly. To ensure that finances comply with the law before public accountants conduct audits, management accountants and internal auditors increasingly will be needed to discover and eliminate fraud. Also, in an effort to make government agencies more efficient and accountable, demand for government accountants should increase.

Other duties may include monitoring and assessing ongoing performance, as well as working on financial and economic planning and analysis. Most workers in this department become specialized in any of a number of areas, resulting in the promotion to another facility or location for general managerial responsibilities.

Another career available to business or industrial and labor relations graduates with advanced degrees is *human resources*. This field covers a wide range of duties, including employment, compensation and benefits, labor relations, career development, and human resource planning.

Other

One unique career opportunity in the petroleum industry is *food preparation*. Drilling companies are usually responsible for hiring a catering company that specializes in feeding rig workers, particularly offshore where menus must be planned in advance and supplies brought in by boat or helicopter. Working for a catering company is ideal for someone who likes to cook but would like a career out of the traditional restaurant or industrial setting.

Petroleum-related companies also employ secretaries, clerks, warehouse personnel, truck drivers and laborers, as well as welders and mechanics. However, because of the general nature of these jobs, there is probably less opportunity in these careers than in a specialized area of the industry. Salaries and training vary from company to company for these general career opportunities.

Research support staff at a number of major oil companies also includes personnel trained in health and safety engineering, entomology, biochemistry, plant pathology, toxicology, mathematics, and statistics. Another important position is the *research scientist*, who studies ways of using chemicals to remove oil from coal, shale, and tar sands. They may also study ways to use other energy sources. Research scientists may be called *chemical engineers* or *technical engineers* and may help look for alternate energy technologies, particularly in recovering and refining petroleum products. For more information, refer to the *Occupational Outlook Handbook* (www.bls.gov/oco); the *Dictionary of Occupational Titles* (www.occupationalinfo.org); and *Career Guide to Industries* (www.bls.gov/oco/cg). More information about employment in Canada can be found at www.jobfutures.ca.

8

Canada's Energy Industry

Canada has considerable natural resources and is one of the world's largest producers and exporters of energy, exporting about 1.4 million barrels per day of crude oil and 10.5 billion cubic feet per day of natural gas, primarily to U.S. markets, according to the Petroleum Human Resources Council of Canada. The country is the world's third-largest producer of natural gas and seventh-largest producer of crude oil.

The Canadian energy industry is a significant contributor to the country's economy as a large employer of Canadians and through direct investment and taxes. The industry accounts for 6 percent of the country's gross domestic product (GDP). The sector provides essential services and wealth and operates in a high-technology environment.

Presently, Canada's entire petroleum industry directly and indirectly employs more than five hundred thousand people, and more than seven thousand new jobs are forecast in the exploration and production segment of the petroleum industry by 2012, according to a study by the Petroleum Human Resources Council of Canada.

Here are other facts that show the significance of the energy industry in Canada:

- More than one-third of the billions spent by the offshore industry go directly into regional and local economies.
- Oil and gas supply and demand are linked together in Canada by seven hundred thousand kilometers of pipelines—long enough to circle the earth seventeen times at the equator.
- In 2003, 33 percent of Canada's crude oil production came from the oil sands. By 2010, oil sands could provide more than 50 percent of Canada's crude oil production.

Employment Opportunities

One of the best sources of information on petroleum employment opportunities in Canada is the Petroleum Human Resources Council, a group supported by eleven oil and gas national and regional industry organizations, including one union. It represents key sectors of the petroleum industry in Canada: exploration, development, production, service industries, pipeline transmission, gas processing and mining, and extracting and upgrading heavy oil and bitumen.

The organization's website—www.petrohrsc.ca—has a wealth of information and links to additional career sites. The following information is from the Petroleum Human Resources Council.

Western Canada Sedimentary Basin

Employment opportunities in western Canada are in the conventional industry that taps the Western Canada Sedimentary Basin

(WCSB), including the areas of Alberta, northwestern Saskatchewan, northeastern British Columbia and parts of Manitoba, the Northwest Territories, and the Yukon Territory.

Labor supply and demand are closely balanced in the Western Canada Sedimentary Basin, and they are expected to remain as such during the next decade. Job opportunities will be affected the most by retirements within the existing workforce, the automation of industry processes, and changing business practices. The greatest opportunities will most likely be in engineering, technology, and operations-related positions.

Engineers (corrosion, electrical, and chemical, among others), technicians (electrical and instrumentation, in particular), and environmental specialists will also be needed.

The Oil Sands

The oil sands region, located primarily in northeastern Alberta and northwestern Saskatchewan, is expected to double its workforce within the next ten years by adding eighty-six hundred new jobs. The workers most in demand are likely to be heavy equipment operators, process operators, heavy-duty mechanics, and power engineers.

Central Canada

There is some energy activity in central Canada, where all sectors are represented to some degree. Although Québec does not have current production, it does have mainline oil and natural gas pipelines. There is also some exploration interest. As most of this exploration is in the eastern portion of the province and is linked geologically to exploration efforts on the East Coast, this analysis of the East Coast is also relevant to Québec.

Ontario, which has produced petroleum continuously since 1858, now accounts for less than 1 percent of the national total but provides more than half of Canada's natural gas storage capacity. The skills needed to find and exploit natural gas storage structures are virtually identical to those of the conventional petroleum exploration and extraction industries.

Like Québec, Ontario also has mainline oil and natural gas pipelines. While the Ontario industry is further along the life-cycle curve than the WCSB, almost all of the human resources issues related to the mature WCSB are directly relevant to Ontario. Therefore, the analysis and discussion of the WCSB can be applied directly to Ontario.

The East Coast

Offshore exploration on the East Coast—those offshore areas under the jurisdiction of Nova Scotia and Newfoundland and Labrador—may result in the creation of as many as forty-five hundred jobs during the next decade. Those with training or experience in the offshore environment will likely benefit most. There may also be excellent opportunities for project managers, some engineers, marine officers, those who specialize in offshore drilling, and other positions such as development drilling personnel.

The North

There is little oil and gas exploration activity in the North—areas that include the Mackenzie Delta, Beaufort Sea Offshore, and onshore areas in northern portions of the Northwest Territories.

Industry employment tends to be restricted to the winter season. Fifty permanent operational positions and two hundred permanent field jobs will be created if a new pipeline is constructed through the Mackenzie Valley during the next decade.

Despite short-term labor pressures for the construction industry, labor supply and demand is likely to be in balance since the number of permanent positions is small.

Labor and Skill Shortages

A March 2007 *Northern Saskatchewan Training Needs Assessment Report* found that the greatest demand in oil production and oil upgrading is in engineering (all disciplines—mechanical, process, mining, electrical, metallurgical, geo-technical, and environmental engineers), technology (electrical, geological, and chemical technicians), and trades (electricians, heavy-duty mechanics, instrument technicians, millwrights, pipe fitters, ironworkers, carpenters, welders). The demand is highest for trade workers with journeyperson status—opportunities increase as apprentices achieve higher levels.

The report noted that oil and gas well drilling creates about twelve thousand jobs in western Canada. At the time of the report, there were about six hundred oil and gas drilling rigs operating in western Canada, with each employing about twenty workers. The majority are located in Alberta, although many are situated in Saskatchewan. From 2005 to 2010, Alberta forecasts there will be 250 to 370 new jobs each year, as well as openings created by employee turnover.

Workers without a high school degree or postsecondary training can still get a job with oil and gas drilling and service contractors—one of the few industries where new employees can still train on the job. New employees start as lease hands or floor hands and later advance to motor hand, derrick hand, and driller positions. Northlands College offers the mandatory pre-employment oil fields safety courses as does Enform Institute (formerly Petroleum Industry Training Service) in Calgary and Nisku (near Edmonton). Mandatory safety courses include H2S Alive certification.

Crews work outdoors, often year-round in remote locations, and are exposed to extremes in weather. Like their U.S. counterparts, they typically work twelve-hour shifts over a two-week period.

(This report was published by Northlands College, the Northern Labour Market Committee, and Saskatchewan Advanced Education and Employment, Northern Office. It can be found on the website of Keewatin Career Development Corporation [http://career.kcdc.ca/kcdc], a nonprofit, umbrella organization of career-service-providing agencies in Northern Saskatchewan.)

Earnings

Canadians who work in oil and gas well drilling occupations earned an average salary C$60,100 a year, according to the 2005 Alberta Wage and Salary Survey. Earnings vary from province to province. Here are a few samples of salaries for positions in the petroleum industry.

In Alberta, *drilling rig managers* may be paid a day rate of about C$600 a day or an hourly rate. Depending on location and hours of operation, *service-rig managers* may be paid a day rate of about C$550 a day or an hourly rate (2005 estimates). According to the 2005 Alberta Wage and Salary Survey, Albertans in the *oil and gas drilling and service supervisor* occupational group working part-time or full-time earned from C$35,900 to C$265,500 a year. The average salary was C$87,600 a year.

According to the 2005 Alberta Wage and Salary Survey, Albertans in the *petroleum, gas, and chemical process operator* occupational group working part-time or full-time earned from C$35,400 to C$115,000 a year. The average salary was C$77,900 a year.

For More Information

For more information on employment in Canada, the following websites are good resources to find out more about jobs in the petroleum industry. Specific Canadian websites include www.petrohrsc.ca/english/links_member.html and www.petrohrsc.ca/english/links_national.html. Many more organization and association websites are located in Appendix A.

Alberta

Alberta Learning Information Service
Employment: www.alis.gov.ab.ca/employment
Occupational profiles: www.alis.gov.ab.ca/occinfo
Earnings information: www.alis.gov.ab.ca/wageinfo

Saskatchewan

SaskNetWork
www.sasknetwork.gov.sk.ca

Keewatin Career Development Corporation
http://career.kcdc.ca/kcdc

9

Employment Outlook for the Future

As we move toward the end of the first decade of the twenty-first century, events across the globe continue to plague the petroleum business—the ongoing war in Iraq, an unstable Middle East, a growing demand for energy in North America, and emerging economies such as India and China.

Global Policies Impact Industry

The petroleum industry has been at the center of world politics for more than a quarter of a century. Even so, two interruptions of Mideast oil supplies—in the mid-1970s and the Gulf War in the early 1990s—did not change how the United States dealt with future energy issues. It is only now, in 2007, that the debate has begun to intensify on what we need to do as a country to have true energy security.

By the spring of 2007, the United States was importing almost 60 percent of the petroleum it consumed. The largest source was Canada. That means most of the crude oil used by Americans today is not produced in the United States but in countries throughout the world. The previous highest level of imports was 48 percent in 1979.

Some of the largest producers of petroleum outside of the United States belong to OPEC—the Organization of Petroleum Exporting Countries. In recent years, when non-OPEC countries increased petroleum production, OPEC lost market share—and a lot of the political clout it carried through the previous decade. When oil dropped to $10 a barrel in 1986, U.S. companies scaled back exploration and production efforts because it was economically unfeasible to compete with foreign governments, who essentially own the oil firms. OPEC still has a firm hold on worldwide energy issues, but its position has substantially weakened in recent years. U.S. policies that would allow for more conservation, such as more fuel-efficient cars, or for an increase in domestic production, continue to be debated.

U.S. production of crude oil fell from 9.6 million barrels a day in 1970 to 5.2 million barrels a day in 2007. On the other hand, U.S.-marketed natural gas production in January 2007 was 53.4 billion cubic feet per day, an increase from January 2006 of 52.5 billion cubic feet per day, according to the U.S. Department of Energy.

Demand for energy—both crude oil and natural gas—continues to grow, however, at a rate of about 1.1 percent a year, with a projected increase of 34.0 percent from 2004 to 2030.

The U.S. Strategic Petroleum Reserve (SPR) is the largest stockpile of government-owned emergency crude oil in the world. Established in the aftermath of the 1973–1974 oil embargo, the SPR provides the U.S. president with a powerful response option should a disruption in commercial oil supplies threaten the U.S. economy. It also allows the United States to meet part of its International Energy Agency obligation to maintain emergency oil stocks, and it provides a national defense fuel reserve.

The Energy Policy Act of 2005 directed the secretary of energy to fill the SPR to its authorized one-billion-barrel capacity. This required the Department of Energy to complete proceedings to select sites necessary to expand the SPR to one billion barrels. For more information on the SPR, go to www.spr.doe.gov.

The petroleum industry funds a large part of government at all levels. From 1980 to 1988, the year a windfall profits tax on the industry was repealed, energy companies paid twice the amount of federal taxes than any other industry. Today, the petroleum industries pay billions of dollars to state and local governments in the form of severance and production taxes.

A Cyclical Industry

The petroleum industry has experienced both booms and busts over the years, illustrating the cyclical relationship between the price of oil and employment. During periods of high oil and gas prices, the industry expands exploration and production and hires more workers. The opposite occurs during periods of low prices.

According to the *Career Guide to Industries*, 2006–2007, the U.S. petroleum industry employed about 316,000 wage and salary workers in 2004. Of these, only four in ten workers were employed directly by the oil and gas extraction companies. The rest worked as contractors in the support activities for the mining sector, which also included workers who extract coal and minerals on a contract basis. Although onshore oil and gas extraction establishments are found in forty-two states, almost three out of four of the industry's workers in 2004 were located in just four states—California, Louisiana, Oklahoma, and Texas. (See Chapter 8 for more information on Canada's energy industry.)

While most workers are employed on land, many work at offshore sites. Although they are not included in employment figures for this industry, many Americans are employed by oil companies at locations in Africa, the North Sea, the Far East, the Middle East, South America, and countries of the former Soviet Union.

Slightly more than 50 percent of establishments employ fewer than five workers; the vast majority of workers are employed in establishments with twenty or more workers. As more large domestic oil fields and gas fields are depleted, major oil companies are focusing their exploration and production activity in foreign countries. Consequently, smaller companies with less capital for foreign exploration and production are drilling an increasing share of domestic oil and gas wells. Technology also has significantly decreased the risk and cost for smaller producers.

Promotion opportunities for some jobs may be limited due to the general decline of the domestic petroleum industry. Advancement opportunities for oil field workers remain best for those with skill and experience. There should continue to be some opportunities for entry-level field crew workers to acquire the skills that qualify them for higher-level jobs within the industry.

Due to the critical nature of the work, offshore crews, even at the entry level, generally are more experienced than land crews. Many companies will not employ someone who has no knowledge of oil field operations to work on an offshore rig, so workers who have gained experience as part of a land crew might advance to offshore operations.

As workers gain knowledge and experience, U.S. or foreign companies operating in other countries also may hire them. Although this can be a lucrative and exciting experience, it may not be suitable for everyone because it usually means leaving family and friends and adapting to different customs and living standards.

Experience gained in many oil and gas extraction jobs also has application in other industries. For example, roustabouts can move to construction jobs, while machinery operators and repairers can transfer to other industries with similar machinery. Geologists and engineers may become involved with environmental activities, especially those related to this industry.

Working Conditions

Working conditions in the industry vary significantly by occupation. Roustabout jobs and jobs in other construction and extraction occupations may involve rugged outdoor work in remote areas in all kinds of weather. For these jobs, physical strength and stamina are necessary. This work involves standing for long periods, lifting moderately heavy objects, and climbing and stooping to work with tools that often are oily and dirty. Executives generally work in office settings, as do most administrators and clerical workers. Geologists, engineers, and managers may split their time between the office and the job sites, particularly while involved in exploration work.

Opportunities for part-time work in this industry are rare. In fact, a higher percentage of workers in oil and gas extraction work overtime than in all other industries. The average nonsupervisory worker in the oil and gas extraction industry worked 43.5 hours per week in 2004, compared with 33.7 hours for all nonsupervisory workers on private nonfarm payrolls.

Oil and gas well drilling and servicing can be hazardous. However, in 2003 the rate of work-related injury and illness in the oil and gas extraction industry was 1.8 per 100 full-time workers and 2.7 for workers in support activities for mining—somewhat lower than the 5.0 for the entire private sector. Improvements in drilling technology and oil rig operations, such as remote-controlled drills, have led to fewer injuries.

Drilling rigs operate continuously. On land, drilling crews usually work six days in a row, eight hours a day, and then have a few days off. In offshore operations, workers can work fourteen days in a row, twelve hours a day, and then have fourteen days off. If the offshore rig is located far from the coast, the drilling crew lives on ships anchored nearby or in facilities on the platform itself. Workers on offshore rigs are always evacuated in the event of a storm. Most workers in oil and gas well operations and maintenance or in natural gas processing work eight hours a day, five days a week.

Many oil field workers are away from home for weeks or months at a time. Exploration field personnel and drilling workers frequently move from place to place as work at a particular field is completed. In contrast, well operation and maintenance workers and natural gas processing workers usually remain in the same location for extended periods.

Job Outlook

Although worldwide demand for oil and gas is expected to grow, overall U.S. wage and salary employment in the oil and gas extraction industry is expected to decline by 6 percent through the year 2014, compared to an employment increase of 14 percent in all industries combined, according to the *Career Guide to Industries*.

In general, the level of future crude petroleum and natural gas exploration and development and, therefore, employment opportunities in this industry remains contingent upon the size of accessible reserves available and whatever the the going prices are for oil and gas. Stable and favorable prices are needed to allow companies enough revenue to expand exploration and production projects to keep pace with growing global energy demand, particularly by India and China.

Rising worldwide demand for oil and gas is likely to cause higher long-term prices and generate the needed incentive to continue exploring and developing oil and gas in this country, at least in the short run. Over the moderate term, fewer reserves of oil and gas in the United States will cause a decline in domestic production, unless new oil and gas fields are found and developed.

Environmental concerns, accompanied by strict regulation and limited access to protected federal lands, also continue to have a major impact on this industry. Restrictions on drilling in environmentally sensitive areas and other environmental constraints should continue to limit exploration and development, both onshore and offshore. However, changes in policy could expand exploration and drilling for oil and natural gas in currently protected areas, especially in Alaska.

In addition, environmental emissions standards already in place or planned for the future are expected to significantly limit the amount of sulfur and carbon dioxide levels that can be emitted by power plants. Employment in the natural gas exploration and production industry normally would grow with the increasing demand for cleaner-burning fuels, such as natural gas. However, high natural gas prices can limit demand and cause some planned future power plants to return to coal as a power source, which could hurt the long-term natural gas outlook.

While some new oil and gas deposits are being discovered in this country, companies increasingly are moving to more lucrative foreign locations. As companies expand into other areas around the globe, the need for employees in the United States is reduced. However, advances in technology have increased the proportion of exploratory wells that yield oil and gas, enhanced offshore exploration and drilling capabilities, and extended the production of existing wells. As a result, more exploration and development ventures are profitable and provide employment opportunities that otherwise would have been lost.

Despite an overall decline in employment in the oil and gas extraction industry, job opportunities in most occupations should remain good. The need to replace workers who transfer to other industries, retire, or leave the workforce will be the major source of job openings as more workers in this industry approach retirement age and others seek more stable employment opportunities in other industries. Employment opportunities will be best for those with previous experience and with technical skills, especially qualified professionals and extraction workers who have significant experience in oil field operations and who can also work with new technology.

More workers will be needed who are capable of using new technologies—such as 3-D and 4-D seismic exploration methods, horizontal and directional drilling techniques, and deepwater and subsea technologies—as employers develop and implement sophisticated new equipment.

Earnings

Average wage and salary earnings in the oil and gas extraction industry were significantly higher than the average for all industries. The average hourly earnings of nonsupervisory workers in the oil and gas extraction sector were $18.58 and $16.92 for workers in the support activities for mining, compared with $15.67 for all workers in private industry.

Due to the working conditions, employees at offshore operations generally earn higher wages than do workers at onshore oil fields. College-educated workers and technical-school graduates in professional and technical occupations usually earn the most.

Few industry workers belong to unions. In fact, only about 5 percent of workers were union members or were covered by union contracts in 2004, compared with about 14 percent of all workers throughout private industry.

Preparing for a Future in the Petroleum Industry

If you're still in high school, a good place to begin is with your guidance counselor. Your skills and aptitudes already should have been analyzed through a variety of standard examinations. These should give you a clear idea of the areas in which you already excel. For any career route you take, don't forget that the basics of reading, writing, and arithmetic are important, as is proficiency with computers. Companies require that employees have an absolute minimum of a high school diploma or GED equivalent.

If you're leaning toward a professional career in the petroleum industry that requires a college degree, you should study courses in high school that will prepare you for a tougher college curriculum.

For instance, future engineers should take as many science and math courses as possible.

You should begin to inquire about entrance requirements to colleges and universities that specialize in petroleum-related fields. Be sure it is in an area of the country that you will be happy living in and one that you can afford. Educational institutions that specialize in petroleum and related curriculums are listed in Appendix B.

Many local chapters of national and international petroleum organizations and associations award scholarships to high school graduates as well as college freshmen in a particular petroleum discipline. For a list of cities with local chapters, contact the associations and organizations listed in Appendix A.

If you're interested in learning a specific trade, there are a number of both private and public vocational-technical schools that offer a variety of courses that would be applicable to a career in the petroleum industry. Whether you enter college or a trade school, find out as much as you can about the school by talking to a recent graduate to learn about the school's reputation in that particular field.

Occasionally, there are jobs that provide on-the-job training. This is the way a number of companies hire various types of personnel, including laborers, clerks, and secretaries, for example. Many of them also provide in-house training for a particular job and opportunities for advancement.

Adults who want to change careers but cannot afford to leave their present job may want to consider taking evening courses through an adult education program. Many cities offer weekend or night programs for adults. Others living in a college town may want to consider obtaining another degree or completing a degree.

In some energy towns, colleges and trade schools design curriculum around an oil field worker's seven-and-seven schedule. You may want to consider taking a job that caters to this schedule. This would enable you to continue working while furthering your education at the same time.

Contact others in your field of interest and ask them to recommend training programs. Other sources of information include trade journals, the commercial listings in your telephone book, and local and state boards of education.

Looking for a Job

If you're about to complete your college studies, one of the best places to start is the placement office at your university. Because energy companies use a variety of personnel in their daily operations, many like to recruit recent college graduates. Energy companies contact placement offices and schedule time for the company recruiter to visit the campus. You will need to schedule an appointment with the recruiter prior to the visit.

Keep in touch with your curriculum advisors via e-mail. They may come across opportunities not initially available to you. Even if you're out of school, you may be able to register with the placement office at your alma mater. A number of schools allow their graduates to register with the placement office, and alumni are matched to companies seeking employees.

Another good job-hunting source is the local chapter of trade organizations or professional societies. Members are in touch with others in the industry and may hear of openings that fit your education and training. Some associations have student chapters on campus, and some include job postings on their websites. A list of organizations is provided in Appendix A.

Internet sites that cater to job searches (such as www.monster.com or www.careerbuilder.com) are also excellent sources of job listings. Many cities also have their own sites, so be sure to use the Internet as a resource during your job search. There are numerous other websites that cater specifically to the energy industry, so use your favorite search engine to search for jobs in the energy sector. Some of these special energy job sites also are listed in Appendix A.

The classified section of daily newspapers is another option for job seekers. Many companies advertise in the state's largest newspaper or in the publication located near the area's energy center.

A head-hunting agency is usually hired by an employer seeking a special type of person in a particular field. This worker is usually already employed, and the agency attempts to woo him or her away. Fees to head-hunting agencies are almost always paid by the employer.

The U.S. Department of Labor and state and provincial employment services have offices in major cities, and this is another option when job hunting. Check on other city or county services that may be offered in your particular area.

Other ways of getting information on jobs include talking to a recognized expert in the field or a management consultant, the local chamber of commerce, and others who have recently graduated in your curriculum and have found jobs. Also, attend petroleum exhibits and conferences that attract top executives from the industry. One of the largest shows is the Offshore Technology Conference in Houston, Texas, which attracts hundreds of oil company exhibitors from all over the world. Thousands of visitors attend the conference, which is held each year in early May. In Lafayette,

Louisiana, the Louisiana Gulf Coast Oil Exposition is held in odd-numbered years and features new offshore technology. A similar show in Odessa, Texas, in even-numbered years, showcases new onshore advancements. Other shows are held periodically throughout the United States and the world.

Although it is a good idea to contact company personnel departments, you can also call company department heads directly and ask for an interview. These managers usually know before the personnel department whether an opening is anticipated. Do your homework, and have a short statement prepared on how you can help the company. If talking to the personnel department, ask about sending your résumé to keep on file. Also, ask about a summer job or internship program.

A Final Word

Times have changed since your parents and grandparents entered the workforce. Workers of their day typically selected a career and remained in the same field—sometimes with the same company—until they reached retirement age. Today, career experts predict that most of us will change careers several times during our lifetimes.

We live in a global world and are faced with increased competition from other countries. In many cases, it is politics, not economics, that plays a major role in industrial competitiveness. When that happens, we may not have control over our careers.

If you plan on making the petroleum industry a lifelong career, keep in mind the cyclical nature of the business. A personality to cope with the industry's ups and downs is crucial to survival, as is being financially prepared to weather the expected boom-to-bust cycles.

Lack of a U.S. energy policy and continued dependence on foreign oil sources add to the uncertainty of this industry. However, with fields of oil and natural gas left to be discovered, the entry of liquefied natural gas (LNG) expected to reach the United States via tanker, a growing population throughout the world, and an increasing demand for energy, there is expected to be a market for petroleum workers—at least in the foreseeable future.

Appendix A

Key Job-Search Websites, Organizations, and Associations

Thanks to the Internet, there is a wealth of information that allows you to thoroughly research career choices at home or in your school or public library. The growth of online listings has made a wide variety of resources available at your fingertips. Companies, professional societies, academic institutions, and government agencies maintain a presence on the Internet with regular updates that include the most current information.

The Internet has information such as government documents, schedules of events, job openings, and even networking contacts. Listings for academic institutions provide links to career counseling and placement services through career resource centers, as well as information on financing your education. Colleges and universities also offer online guides to campus facilities and admission requirements and procedures.

The variety of career information databases available through the Internet provides much of the same information available through libraries, career centers, and guidance offices. However, no single network or resource will contain all the desired information, so be prepared to use numerous resources when researching career choices. The *Occupational Outlook Handbook* recommends that, as in a library search, a researcher must look through various lists by field or discipline or use particular keywords.

The following websites, organizations, and associations in the United States and Canada may be contacted for further information about the petroleum industry and available careers. Be prepared to spend a lot of time researching links to other sites and for Web addresses to change without notice. You can also visit http://pweb.netcom.com/~jsharry/geolsite.html to browse a wide array of Internet sites for the petroleum industry.

Key Job-Search Websites

Career Guide to Industries
Bureau of Labor Statistics
www.bls.gov/oco/cg

Directory of Occupational Titles
www.occupationalinfo.org

Earthworks Energy Jobs Database
www.earthworks-jobs.com

JETS-Guidance
Junior Engineering Technical Society
www.jets/org/publications/guidance.cfm

Job Monkey
www.jobmonkey.com/oilindustry

Making it Count
www.makingitcount.com/energyapi

Occupational Information Network (O*NET)
www.occupationalinfo.org/onet

Occupational Outlook Handbook
Bureau of Labor Statistics
www.bls.gov/oco/htm

Occupational Outlook Quarterly
http://stats.bls.gov/opub/ooq/ooqhome.htm

Oil Careers
www.oilcareers.com

PennEnergy Jobs
www.pennenergyjobs.com

University of Houston
www.uh.edu/~jbutler/geophysics/org.htm

Worldwide Worker
www.worldwideworker.com

Government and Petroleum-Related Organizations and Associations

American Association of Drilling Engineers
AADE–National
P.O. Box 940069
Houston, TX 77094
www.aade.org

American Association of Petroleum Geologists
P.O. Box 979
Tulsa, OK 74101-0979
www.aapg.org

American Chemical Society
1155 Sixteenth St. NW
Washington, DC 20036
www.acs.org

American Congress on Surveying and Mapping
6 Montgomery Village Ave., Ste. 403
Gaithersburg, MD 20879
www.acsm.net

American Gas Association
400 N. Capitol St. NW, Ste. 400
Washington, DC 20001
www.aga.org

American Geological Institute
4220 King St.
Alexandria, VA 22302-1502
www.agiweb.org

American Geophysical Union
2000 Florida Ave. NW
Washington, DC 20009-1277
www.agu.org

American Institute of Chemical Engineers
3 Park Ave.
New York, NY 10016-5991
www.aiche.org

American Institute of Mining, Metallurgical,
and Petroleum Engineers
P.O. Box 270728
Littleton, CO 80127-0013
www.aimeny.org

American Petroleum Institute
1220 L St. NW
Washington, DC 20005-4070
www.api.org
www.adventuresinenergy.org
www.classroom-energy.org
www.energyprofessions.org
www.energytomorrow.org

American Society for Photogrammetry and Remote Sensing
5410 Grosvenor La., Ste. 210
Bethesda, MD 20814-2160
www.asprs.org

American Society of Professional Landmen
4100 Fossil Creek Blvd.
Fort Worth, TX 76137
www.landman.org

American Society for Testing and Materials
100 Barr Harbor Dr.
West Conshohocken, PA 19428-2959
www.astm.org

American Welding Society
550 NW LeJeune Rd.
Miami, Florida 33126
www.aws.org

Association of Energy Service Companies
10200 Richmond Ave., Ste. 275
Houston, Texas 77042
www.aesc.net

Canadian Association of Geophysical Contractors
1045, 1015 Fourth St. SW
Calgary, AB T2R 1J4
Canada
www.cagc.ca

Canadian Association of Oilwell Drilling Contractors
800, 540 Fifth Ave. SW
Calgary, AB T2P 0M2
Canada
www.caodc.ca

Canadian Association of Petroleum Producers, Ste. 2100
350 Seventh Ave. SW
Calgary, AB T2P 3N9
Canada
www.capp.ca

Canadian Centre for Energy Information, Ste. 1600
800 Sixth Ave. SW
Calgary, AB T2P 3G3
Canada
www.centreforenergy.com

Canadian Energy Pipeline Association
1860, 205 Fifth Ave. SW
Calgary, AB T2P 2V7
Canada
www.cepa.com

Canadian Institute of Mining, Metallurgy, and Petroleum, Ste. 855
3400 de Maisonneuve Blvd. W
Montreal, QC H3Z 3B8
Canada
www.cim.org

Canadian Society of Exploration Geophysicists (CSEG), No. 600
640 Eighth Ave. SW
Calgary, AB T2P 1G7
Canada
www.cseg.ca

Canadian Society of Petroleum Geologists
600, 640 Eighth Ave. SW
Calgary, AB T2P 1G7
Canada
www.cspg.org

Council of Petroleum Accountants Societies
3900 E. Mexico Ave., Ste. 602
Denver, CO 80210
www.copas.org

Drilling Engineering Association
www.dea-global.org

Energy Information Administration
1000 Independence Ave., SW
Washington, DC 20585
www.eia.doe.gov

Energy Institute
61 New Cavendish St.
London W1G 7AR
United Kingdom
www.energyinst.org.uk

Enform
1538 Twenty-Fifth Ave. NE
Calgary, AB T2E 8Y3
Canada
www.enform.ca

Engineers Canada
180 Elgin St., Ste. 1100
Ottawa, ON K2P 2K3
Canada
engineerscanada.ca

Gas Processing Association Canada
900 Sixth Ave. SW, Ste. 505
Calgary, AB T2P 3K2
Canada
www.gpacanada.com

Gas Processors Association
6526 E. 60th St.
Tulsa, OK 74145
www.gasprocessors.com

Government of Canada–Human Resources and
Social Development Canada
www.hrsdc.gc.ca

Government of Canada–Service Canada
Publications Centre
Human Resources Development Canada
140 Promenade du Portage, Phase IV
Hull, QC K1A 0J9
Canada
www.jobfutures.ca

Independent Petroleum Association of America
1201 Fifteenth St. NW, Ste. 300
Washington, DC 20005
www.ipaa.org

International Association of Drilling Contractors
P.O. Box 4287
Houston, TX 77210-4287
www.iadc.org

International Right of Way Association
19750 S. Vermont Ave., Ste. 220
Torrance, CA 90502-1144
www.irwaonline.org

Interstate Natural Gas Association of America
10 G St. NE, Ste. 700
Washington, DC 20002
www.ingaa.org

Intervention and Coiled Tubing Association
P.O. Box 1082
Montgomery, TX 77356
www.icota.com

Junior Engineering Technical Society
1420 King St., Ste. 405
Alexandria, VA 22314
www.jets.org

Louisiana Mid-Continent Oil and Gas Association
801 North Blvd.
Baton Rouge, LA 70802
www.lmoga.com

Marine Technology Society
5565 Sterrett Pl., Ste. 108
Columbia, MD 21044
www.mtsociety.org

National Association of Corrosion Engineers
1440 South Creek Dr.
Houston, TX 77084-4906
www.nace.org

National Association of Energy Service Companies
1615 M St. NW, Ste. 800
Washington, DC 20036
www.naesco.org

National Society of Professional Engineers
1420 King St.
Alexandria, VA 22314-2794
www.nspe.org

Natural Gas Supply Association
805 Fifteenth St. NW, Ste. 510
Washington, DC 20005
www.ngsa.org
www.naturalgas.org

Newfoundland Ocean Industries Association, Ste. 602
Atlantic Pl., 215 Water St.
St. John's, NF A1C 6C9
www.noianet.com

Offshore Technology
SPG Media Limited
Brunel House
55–57 N. Wharf Rd.
London W2 1LA
United Kingdom
www.offshore-technology.com

Oil and Gas Journal
1700 W. Loop South, Ste. 1000
Houston, TX 77027
www.ogj.com

Oil and Gas Online
5340 Fryling Rd., Ste. 101
Erie, PA 16510
www.oilandgasonline.com

Oil Online
Atlantic Communications
1635 W. Alabama
Houston, TX 77006-4196
www.oilonline.com/gcod

Ontario Petroleum Institute
555 Southdale Rd. East, Ste. 104
London, ON N6E 1A2
Canada
www.ontpet.com

Petroleum Extension Service
The University of Texas at Austin
Petroleum Extension Service
1 University Station, R8100
Austin, TX 78712-1100
www.utexas.edu/ce/petex

Petroleum Human Resources Council, Ste. 410
800 Sixth Ave. SW
Calgary, AB T2P 3G3
www.petrohrsc.ca

Petroleum Services Association of Canada, Ste. 1150
800 Sixth Ave. SW
Calgary, AB T2P 3G3
www.psac.ca
www.careersinoilandgas.com

Petroleum Technology Transfer Council
P.O. Box 246
Sand Springs, OK 74063
www.pttc.org

Rocky Mountain Mineral Law Foundation
9191 Sheridan Blvd., Ste. 203
Westminster, CO 80031
www.rmmlf.org

Small Explorers and Producers Association of Canada,
1060, 717 Seventh Ave. SW
Calgary, AB T2P 0Z3
www.sepac.ca

Society of Exploration Geophysicists
8801 S. Yale
Tulsa, OK 74137-3575
www.seg.org

Society of Petroleum Engineers
P.O. Box 833836
Richardson, TX 75083-3836
www.spe.org

Society of Petrophysicists and Well Log Analysts
8866 Gulf Freeway, Ste. 320
Houston, TX 77017
www.spwla.org

Texas Independent Producers and Royalty Owners Association
919 Congress Ave., Ste. 1000
Austin, TX 78701
www.tipro.org

U.S. Bureau of Labor Statistics
Office of Occupational Statistics and Employment Projections
2 Massachusetts Ave. NE, Ste. 2135
Washington, DC 20212-0001
www.bls.gov/oco
http://stats.bls.gov/opub/ooq/ooqhome.htm

U.S. Department of Energy
1000 Independence Ave., SW
Washington, DC 20585
www.energy.gov

U.S. Department of the Interior
U.S. Geological Survey
Reston, VA 20192
http://geology.er.usgs.gov/eastern/careers.html

U.S. Department of the Interior Minerals Management Service
1849 C St. NW
Washington, DC 20240
www.mms.gov

Appendix B

Schools Specializing in Petroleum and Related Curriculums

In the United States and Canada, numerous colleges, universities, technical schools, and other educational institutions offer a wide range of petroleum engineering or related technical disciplines that are applicable to many facets of the petroleum industry.

Alaska

University of Alaska
425 Duckering Bldg.
P.O. Box 755880
Fairbanks, AK 99775-5880
www.uaf.edu

Alberta

Northern AB Institute of Technology
11762-106 St.
Edmonton, AB T5G 2R1
Canada
www.nait.ca

Southern AB Institute of Technology
Energy and Natural Resources
1301 Sixteenth Ave. NW
Calgary, AB T2M 0L4
Canada
www.sait.ca

University of Alberta
School of Mining and Petroleum Engineering
220 Civil Bldg.
Edmonton, AB T6G 2G6
Canada
www.civil.uAB.ca/petroleum

University of Calgary
2500 University Dr. NW
Calgary, AB T2N 1N4
Canada
www.ucalgary.ca

California

California Polytechnic State University
Petroleum and Mechanical Engineering Department
3801 W. Temple Ave.
Pomona, CA 91768
www.csupomona.edu

California Polytechnic State University
Mechanical and Aeronautical Engineering Department
San Louis Obispo, CA 93407
www.calpoly.edu

California State University
Department of Mechanical Engineering
1250 Bellflower Blvd.
Long Beach, CA 90840-8305
www.csulb.edu

Stanford University
Department of Petroleum Engineering
367 Panama St.
Green Earth Sciences Bldg., Rm. 065
Stanford, CA 94305-2220
http://ekofisk.stanford.edu

University of California
Petroleum Engineering Department
Hearst Mining Bldg.
Berkeley, CA 94720
www.berkeley.edu

University of Southern California
Petroleum Engineering Program
925 Bloom Walk, HED 216
Los Angeles, CA 90089-1211
http://chems.usc.edu/admission/petroleum_engineering.htm

Colorado

Colorado School of Mines
Petroleum Engineering Department
1500 Illinois St.
Golden, CO 80401
www.mines.edu/academic/petroleum

Kansas

University of Kansas
Department of Chemical and Petroleum Engineering
School of Engineering
4006 Learned Hall
Lawrence, KS 66045-2223
www.ku.edu

Louisiana

Louisiana State University
Craft and Hawkins Department of Petroleum Engineering
CEBA Bldg., Rm. 3527
Baton Rouge, LA 70803
www.pete.lsu.edu

Louisiana Tech University
Ruston, LA 71272
www.latech.edu

University of Louisiana
P.O. Box 44690
Lafayette, LA 70504-4690
http://engr.louisiana.edu/pete

Mississippi

Mississippi State University
Box 9544
250 McCain Hall
Mississippi State, MS 39762
www.bagley.msstate.edu

Missouri

University of Missouri
Petroleum Engineering
129 McNutt Hall
Rolla, MO 65409-0420
www.umr.edu/~pet-eng

Montana

Montana Tech of the University of Montana
Department of Petroleum Engineering
1300 W. Park St.
Butte, MT 59701
www.mtech.edu

Newfoundland

College of the North Atlantic
Ridge Road Campus
P.O. Box 1150
St. John's, NF A1A 6L8
Canada
www.cna.nl.ca

Memorial University of Newfoundland
Engineering and Applied Science
St. John's, NF A1B 3X5
Canada
www.mun.ca

New Mexico

New Mexico Tech
801 Leroy Pl.
MSEC 300A
Socorro, NM 87801
www.nmt.edu/~petro

Nova Scotia

Atlantic Petroleum Training College
40 Mount Hope Ave.
Dartmouth, NS B2Y 4K9
Canada
www.aptcollege.com

Dalhousie University
Faculty of Engineering
1360 Barrington St.
P.O. Box 1000
Halifax, NS B3J 2X4
Canada
www.dal.ca/engineering/oilandgas

Ohio

Marietta College
Department of Petroleum Engineering
201 Brown Bldg.
215 Fifth St.
Marietta, OH 45750-4017
www.marietta.edu

Oklahoma

University of Oklahoma
Mewbourne School of Petroleum and Geological Engineering
10 E. Boyd Sarkeys Energy Center, Rm. T-301
Norman, OK 73019
www.ou.edu/mewbourneschool

University of Tulsa
Department of Petroleum Engineering
600 S. College Ave.
Tulsa, OK 74104
www.pe.utulsa.edu

Pennsylvania

Penn State University
Petroleum and Natural Gas Engineering
115 Hosler Bldg.
University Park, PA 16802
www.psu.edu

University of Pittsburgh
1249 Benedum Hall
Pittsburgh, PA 15261
www.pitt.edu

Saskatchewan

University of Regina
3737 Wascana Pkwy.
Regina, SK S4S 0A2
Canada
http://enggdynamic.uregina.ca

University of Saskatchewan
57 Campus Dr.
Saskatoon, SK S7N 5A9
Canada
www.usask.ca

South Dakota

South Dakota School of Mines
Department of Geological Engineering
501 E. St. Joseph St.
Rapid City, SD 57701
http://sdmines.sdsmt.edu

Texas

Texas A&M University
Dept. of Petroleum Engineering
3116 TAMU
College Station, TX 77845-3116
http://pumpjack.tamu.edu

Texas A&M University
Chemical and Natural Gas Engineering
Campus Box 193
Kingsville, TX 78363
www.engineer.tamuk.edu/departments/chen/ug.html

Texas Tech University
Eighth and Canton Ave.
Box 43111
Lubbock, TX 79409-3111
www.pe.ttu.edu

University of Houston
Cullen College of Engineering
E421 Engineering Bldg. 2
Houston, TX 77204-4007
www.egr.uh.edu

University of Texas at Austin
Petroleum and Geosystems Engineering
1 University Station C0300
Austin, TX 78712-0228
www.pge.utexas.edu

West Virginia

West Virginia University
College of Engineering and Mineral Resources
Department of Petroleum and Natural Gas Engineering
347 Mineral Resources Bldg.
P.O. Box 6070
Morgantown, WV 26506-6070
www.pnge.cemr.wvu.edu

Wyoming

University of Wyoming
Department of Chemical and Petroleum Engineering
Dept. 3295
1000 E. University Ave.
Laramie, WY 82071
www.eng.uwyo.edu/chemical

Glossary

LIKE MOST INDUSTRIES, the petroleum field has its own language. While many more words and phrases are used in the everyday business of searching for petroleum than are listed here, this glossary is designed to help you better understand the industry.

Many of these terms are from a booklet previously published by the American Petroleum Institute (www.api.org). It is no longer available, but a comprehensive glossary related to the natural gas industry is available online at the Interstate Natural Gas Association of America (www.ingaa.org). Other glossaries are available on other sites, such as the Society of Petroleum Engineers (www.spe.org) and the U.S. Energy Information Administration (www.eia.doe.gov).

Not all the words listed here are included in the preceding chapters. For more details on any of the subjects, check your local library or contact the appropriate organization listed in Appendix A.

Acid rain Acidity in rain or snow produced when carbon, nitrogen, and sulfur compounds oxidize in the atmosphere.

Active solar A system in which mechanical or electrical devices are used to transform solar energy into heat for space heating or other useful energy products. Contrasts with passive solar.

Allocation controls Government policy that specifies quantities of goods or services that potential customers may purchase. Also may designate specific suppliers for such purchases. Crude oil and petroleum products were subject to federal allocation controls through most of the 1970s.

Anthracite coal A variety of coal with a very high heat content (22–28 million Btu per ton). U.S. production is primarily in northeastern Pennsylvania. It once was prized for home heating due to its low content of ash and other impurities. Also called *hard coal.*

Aquifer Underground water reservoir contained between layers of rock, sand, or gravel.

Arab Oil Embargo of 1973–74 During the Arab-Israeli War in October 1973, Arab oil-producing nations agreed to cut off oil shipments to the United States and the Netherlands because they supported Israel. Arab producers simultaneously reduced output. In practice, the shortfall was spread among all oil-importing nations. World prices moved sharply higher. Price and allocation controls suppressed some of the decrease in the United States, but they nevertheless led to gasoline lines.

Areas of Critical Environmental Concern Areas designated by the U.S. Department of the Interior to have historic, cultural, scenic, or natural value that requires protection.

Backfitting (or retrofitting) Modifying equipment to make changes or add features that have been included in later models.

Baghouse An air-filtering device that removes particulates such as carbon from furnaces and process-unit exhausts.

Balance of payments A tabulation of a nation's transactions with the rest of the world that shows the extent to which domestic goods, services, and assets have been transferred to foreign countries and vice versa.

Balance of trade The difference between receipts from foreigners for a nation's goods and services and payments to foreigners for imported goods and services.

Barrel The standard measurement in the oil industry. A barrel of oil equals forty-two U.S. gallons. The measurement originates from the wooden barrels used to transport oil in the early days of oil production.

Basin A depression in the earth in which sedimentary materials have accumulated over a long period of time. A basin may contain many oil or gas fields.

Bcf Billion cubic feet. The cubic foot is a standard unit of measure for quantities of gas at atmospheric pressure.

Benchmark price A benchmark is a standard by which things may be measured. A frequently used benchmark price of oil is the price set by OPEC for Arabian Light crude oil, a 34-degree gravity oil produced in Saudi Arabia. The other OPEC nations set their official prices in accordance with agreed differentials from the benchmark price. In the United States, the most commonly used is West Texas Intermediate.

Best Available Control Technology (BACT) The maximum degree of emissions control that a permitting authority determines to be achievable, considering energy, environmental, and economic impact as well as other costs.

Biomass Any kind of organic substance that can be turned into fuel, such as wood, dry plants, and organic wastes.

Bituminous coal A variety of coal with high heat content (19–30 million Btu per ton) soft enough to be easily ground for combustion. The most widely mined and consumed coal. Also called *soft coal.*

Bonus payment Cash paid to a landowner or other holder of mineral rights by the successful bidder on a mineral lease in addition to any rental or royalty obligations specified in the lease. Many sales of oil and gas leases on federal lands (onshore or offshore) involve bonus payments.

Btu British thermal unit. A standard measure of heat content in a substance that can be burned to provide energy, such as oil, gas, or coal. One Btu equals the amount of energy required to raise the temperature of one pound of water 1 degree Fahrenheit at or near 39.2 degrees Fahrenheit.

Carbon monoxide emissions Colorless, odorless toxic gas sent into the air when carbon molecules are burned incompletely. Nearly all forms of fossil fuel combustion emit carbon oxides.

Certificate of Public Convenience and Necessity Permit issued by FERC under Section 7(c) of the NGA allowing pipelines to engage in the transportation, storage, exchange, or sale for resale of natural gas in interstate commerce or to construct and operate facilities.

Climate change Refers to the variation in the earth's global climate or in regional climates over time and describes changes in the variability or average state of the atmosphere over time scales ranging from decades to millions of years. These changes can be caused by processes internal to the earth, external forces (for example, variations in sunlight intensity) or, more recently, human activities. In recent usage, especially in the context of environmental policy, the term *climate change* often refers only to changes in modern climate, including the rise in average surface temperature known as *global warming*. In some cases, the term is also used with a presumption of human causation, as in the United Nations Framework Convention on Climate Change (UNFCCC). The UNFCCC uses *climate variability* for nonhuman-caused variations.

Cartel Originally a combination of commercial enterprises that formally agree to limit competition by setting prices (often accompanied by output quotas). The term now refers to any group of enterprises that are suspected or accused of anticompetitive behavior. The Organization of Petroleum Exporting Countries (OPEC) has attempted to act as a cartel in the original sense.

Clean Air Act The comprehensive federal law that regulates air emissions from area, stationary, and mobile sources. This law authorizes the U.S. Environmental Protection Agency to establish National Ambient Air Quality Standards (NAAQS) to protect public health and the environment. The goal of the act was to set and achieve NAAQS in every state by 1975. The setting of maximum pollutant standards was coupled with directing the states to develop state implementation plans (SIPs) applicable to appropriate industrial sources in the state. The act was amended in 1977 primarily to set new goals (dates) for achieving attainment of NAAQS because many areas of the country had failed to meet the deadlines. The 1990 amendments to the Clean Air Act in large part were intended to meet unaddressed or insufficiently addressed problems such as acid rain, ground-level ozone, stratospheric ozone depletion, and air toxics.

Coal gasification The chemical conversion of coal to synthetic gaseous fuels.

Coal liquefaction The chemical conversion of coal to synthetic liquid fuels. See also *direct* and *indirect coal liquefaction*.

Coal slurry pipeline A pipeline used to transport coal long distances by mixing crushed coal with water and sending the liquid mixture (or slurry) through pipelines.

Coal washing Cleaning coal with water and certain additives before burning to remove some of the impurities. Most impurities tend to be heavier than coal and sink to the bottom of the water mixture, so the clean coal can be floated off.

Cogeneration The combined production of electrical or mechanical energy and usable heat energy.

Completed well A well made ready to produce oil or natural gas. Completion involves cleaning out the well, running steel casing and tubing in the hole, adding permanent surface control equipment, and perforating the casing so oil or gas can flow into the well and be brought to the surface.

Conventional sources of energy Usually refers to oil, gas, and coal (and sometimes nuclear power) as contrasted with alternative energy sources such as solar, hydro, and geothermal power, synfuels, and various forms of biomass energy.

Core Samples of any subsurface rocks taken as a well is being drilled.

Crude oil equivalent A measure of energy content that converts units of different kinds of energy into the energy equivalent of barrels of oil.

Cushion In discussions of natural gas, refers to the effects of a supply of low-cost, price-controlled gas. The Natural Gas Policy Act of 1978 set up an array of categories of natural gas, some of which are controlled at very low prices. A pipeline that has access to large amounts of this low-cost gas is said to have a deep cushion. This cushion could be used to pay above-market prices for other categories of gas and still enable the pipeline to sell gas at prevailing market prices.

Decontrol Removing government controls on prices and other factors of market activity. Price controls on crude oil began in 1971 and were phased out beginning in 1979. Controls on crude oil ended on January 28, 1981.

Deepwater port A marine terminal constructed offshore to accommodate large vessels, in particular large tankers. The terminal is connected to the shore by submerged pipelines.

Demand The quantity of goods or services that an individual or group wants to buy at a given price.

Development well A well drilled in an already discovered oil or gas field.

Direct coal liquefaction A process by which liquid fuels are produced from the interaction of coal and hydrogen at high temperature and pressure.

Distillate A generic term for several petroleum fuels that are heavier than gasoline and lighter than residual fuels. Home heating oil, diesel, and jet fuels are the most common types of distillate fuels.

Distributor A wholesaler of gasoline and other petroleum products. Also known as a jobber. For natural gas, the distributor is almost always a regulated utility company.

Domestic production Oil and gas produced in the United States in contrast to imported supplies.

Downstream When referring to the oil and gas industry, this term indicates the refining and marketing sectors of the industry. More generically, the term can be used to refer to any step further along in the process.

Drill bit The part of the drilling tool that cuts through rock strata.

Drill string Lengths of steel tubing screwed together to form a pipe connecting the drill bit to the drilling rig. The string is rotated to drill the hole and also serves as a conduit for drilling mud. Also called the drill pipe or drill stem.

Drilling mud An emulsion of water, clays, chemical additives, and weighting materials that flushes rock cuttings from a well, lubricates and cools the drill bit, and maintains the required pressure at the bottom of the well. Examination of cuttings returned to the surface helps geologists evaluate underground rock formations.

Drilling rig The surface equipment used to drill for oil or gas consisting chiefly of a derrick, a winch for lifting and lowering drill pipe, a rotary table to turn the drill pipe, and engines to drive the winch and rotary table.

Dry hole A well that either finds no oil or gas or finds too little to make it financially worthwhile to produce.

Dry natural gas Natural gas containing few or no natural gas liquids (liquid petroleum mixed with gas).

Economic efficiency The absence of waste. If a given commodity can be produced by two techniques, the technique that minimizes cost (an aggregate measure of resources used) per unit of output is more efficient.

Effluent Any waste liquid, gas, or vapor that results from industrial processes. May be harmful to environment unless properly treated.

Electrostatic precipitator A pollution control device that removes particulates from industrial stack emissions, thereby preventing or greatly reducing their discharge into the atmosphere.

Embargo A government order prohibiting commerce. Most frequently a prohibition on exports or imports of a given commodity to or from a nation or nations. See *Arab Oil Embargo of 1973–74*.

Emissions Gases and particulates discharged into the environment, usually the atmosphere.

End-use restrictions A legal prohibition on the use of a certain commodity.

Energy-GNP ratio Amount of energy used to produce a dollar's worth of output, as measured by the gross national product, or GNP.

Enhanced oil recovery Injection of water, steam, gases, or chemicals into underground reservoirs to cause oil to flow toward producing wells, thus permitting more recovery than would have been possible from natural pressure or pumping alone.

Environmental Impact Statement (EIS) A statement of the anticipated effect of a particular action on the environment. An EIS is required of federal agencies by the National Environmental Policy Act of 1969 for any significant action (including granting certain oil and gas permits).

Equilibrium A market situation in which the quantities supplied by sellers matches the quantity demanded by buyers at the current price.

ESECA Energy Supply and Environmental Coordination Act, which was passed in 1974, prohibited certain power plants that had coal-burning capabilities from burning petroleum. It also required any newly constructed fossil fuel boilers to be designed to burn coal.

Ethanol The two-carbon atom alcohol present in the greatest proportion upon the fermentation of grain and other renewable resources such as corn, potatoes, sugar, or timber. It is also called *grain alcohol.*

Excise tax A tax levied on the production, sale, or consumption of a commodity.

Exploratory well A well drilled to an unexplored depth or in unproven territory, either in search of a new reservoir or to extend the known limits of a field that is already partly developed.

Exxon Donor Solvent (EDS) Process A direct coal liquefaction process that dissolves coal in a solvent while adding hydrogen and subjecting it to heat and pressure.

Fault A displacement of subsurface layers of earth or rock that sometimes seals an oil-bearing formation by placing it next to a nonporous formation.

Federal Energy Regulatory Commission (FERC) Federal agency, under the Department of Energy, with jurisdiction over interstate natural gas transportation and sale for resale rates, wholesale electric rates, hydroelectric licensing, oil pipeline rates, and gas pipeline certification. Established in 1977 as successor to the Federal Power Commission.

Federal lands See *government* or *public lands*.

Field A geographical area under which one or more oil or gas reservoirs lie, all of them related to the same geological structure.

Five-year offshore leasing program The first step in the process of leasing offshore lands for oil and gas exploration. The Department of the Interior publishes and annually updates a five-year plan of timetables and areas that will be offered for lease.

Fixed-bed gasification A gasification process in which the raw material is fed as uniform-sized lumps and in which the gas moves through a nearly stationary bed of reacting fuel.

Fluidized bed A bed of fine particles through which a fluid is passed with a velocity high enough for the solid particles to separate and become freely supported in the fluid.

Fly up The possibility of a sudden, sharp increase in prices of natural gas decontrolled in 1985 under the Natural Gas Policy Act of 1978.

Fossil fuels Fuels that originated from the remains of plant, animal, and sea life of previous geological eras. Crude oil, natural gas, coal, shale oil, tar sands, lignite, and peat are all considered fossil fuels.

FUA Powerplant and Industrial Fuel Use Act, passed in 1978, which extended the provisions of ESECA and set specific goals for replacing oil- and gas-burning boilers with coal-fired power.

Geopressured brine Saltwater, unusually hot and in some instances saturated with methane, contained under abnormally high pressure in some sedimentary rocks.

Geothermal energy Energy produced from heat deep in the earth, usually caused by underground water being heated as it flows through hot underground rocks.

Global warming Increase in the average temperature of the earth's near-surface air and oceans in recent decades and its projected continuation.

Glut An excess of supply over demand. In a market system, a glut of a product would cause producers' inventories to increase. The producers would lower the price to bring down their inventories until supply and demand were equal.

GNP (Gross National Product) Total value at market prices of all goods and services produced by the nation's economy. Used as a measure of economic activity.

Government lands Lands owned by the federal government. See *public lands*.

Greenhouse effect The theory that increasing concentrations of carbon dioxide in the atmosphere trap additional heat and moisture and can, in time, create a hothouse effect, raising the temperature of the earth.

Groundwater Water in underground rock strata that supplies wells and springs.

H-coal process A direct coal liquefaction process that adds hydrogen and a catalyst to a coal slurry in a liquefaction vessel.

Heavy oil Crude petroleum characterized by high viscosity and a high carbon-to-hydrogen ratio. It is often difficult to produce heavy oil by conventional techniques, so more costly methods must be used.

Heavy oil sands Rocks containing viscous hydrocarbons (other than coal, oil shale, or tar) that barely flow at reservoir conditions. Hydrocarbons in heavy oil sands flow more readily than those in tar sands but much less readily than those in lighter oil sands.

Hopper car A freight car designed to carry bulk materials such as coal or grain. Its floor slopes to one or more hinged doors for rapid discharge.

Hydrocarbons Any of a large class of organic compounds containing only carbon and hydrogen. The molecular structure of hydrocarbon compounds varies from the simplest, such as methane (CH_4), to heavier and more complex molecules, such as octane (C_8H_{18}), a constituent of crude oil. Crude oil and natural gas often are referred to as hydrocarbons or hydrocarbon fuels.

Hydroelectric power Electric energy produced by harnessing falling water. In most cases, river water flowing through a dam turns a turbine that generates electricity.

In situ In its original place. Refers to methods of producing synfuels underground (underground gasification of a coal seam or heating oil shale underground to release the oil).

Incremental pricing A provision of the Natural Gas Policy Act of 1978 that requires natural gas price increases to be charged to large industrial users instead or residential users, until the price of gas reaches the price of an alternative fuel.

Indirect coal liquefaction A method of making synfuels in which coal is first converted to synthetic gas, then catalyzed to produce hydrocarbons or methanol. Additional processing can convert methanol to gasoline.

Interstate pipeline A pipeline carrying oil or natural gas across state lines. Interstate pipelines are regulated by the federal government.

Intrastate natural gas market The market for natural gas produced and sold for delivery within a state, as opposed to sales across state lines. Intrastate markets had particular significance prior to the passage of the Natural Gas Policy Act of 1978. Until that time, they were not regulated by the federal government, so prices reflected supply and demand rather than federal regulators' decisions.

Iranian cutoff Sharp reductions of Iranian oil supplies in world markets that are due to the events surrounding the 1979 Iranian revolution.

Kerogen The hydrocarbon in oil shales.

Lease offering Also called lease sale. An area of land offered for lease usually by the U.S. Department of the Interior for the exploration for and production of specific natural resources, such as oil and gas. An oil or gas lease conveys no title or occupancy rights, apart from the right to look for and produce petroleum subject to the conditions stated in the lease.

Lignite (or lignite coal) A solid fuel of a higher grade than peat but a lower grade than bituminous coal. Lignite has a high content of moisture and volatile gases. Thus it is soft and has a relatively low heat content, at most 16.5 million Btu per ton.

Liquefied natural gas (LNG) Natural gas that has been converted to a liquid by reducing its temperature to minus 260 degrees Fahrenheit at atmospheric pressure. Gas shipped by seagoing tankers is liquefied before being pumped into the ships and is regasified for pipeline transportation upon reaching its destination.

Liquefied petroleum gases (LPG) Hydrocarbon fractions lighter than gasoline, such as ethane, propane, and butane. They are kept in a liquid state through compression and/or refrigeration and are marketed for various industrial and domestic gas uses. Commonly referred to as bottled gas.

Market A context in which goods are bought and sold, not necessarily confined to a particular geographic location.

Market forces Pressures produced by the free play of supply and demand in a competitive market that induce adjustments in prices and quantities sold.

Market system An economy that relies on market forces to allocate scarce resources, determine production techniques, and price and distribute goods and services. Also referred to as a *price system.*

Mbde Million barrels a day of oil equivalent.

Metallurgical coal A quality of coal used for making coke and steel. Low in ash and sulfur and strong enough to withstand handling. Usually composed of a blend of two grades of bituminous coal. Also called coking coal.

Methanation The final step in high-Btu gas production in which hydrogen-rich gas reacts with carbon monoxide in the presence of a catalyst to form methane.

Methane A light, odorless, flammable gas that is the chief constituent of natural gas.

Methanol A one-carbon atom alcohol made from natural gas, coal, or biomass. Also called *methyl* or *wood alcohol.*

Midstream A term sometimes used to refer to those industry activities that fall between exploration and production (upstream) and refining and marketing (downstream). The term is most often applied to pipeline transportation of crude oil and natural gas.

Miscible flooding An enhanced recovery method in which a fluid, usually carbon dioxide, is injected into a well and dissolves in the oil, which then flows more easily to producing wells. Miscible substances will mix together to form a homogeneous mixture.

Mmcf Million cubic feet. The cubic foot is a standard unit of measure for quantities of gas at the atmosphere pressure.

Moratorium A formally announced suspension of a given type of activity, which can come either at the initiative of the organization(s) concerned or through the intervention of a legal authority.

National Ambient Air Quality Standards Standards in the Clean Air Act that set maximum concentrations that should be allowed nationwide for air pollutants. Standards have been set for seven pollutants: carbon monoxide, hydrocarbons, lead, nitrogen dioxide, ozone, particulates, and sulfur dioxide.

National Energy Policy Act of 1992 A multifaceted energy statute that is intended to reduce U.S. dependence on oil imports. Among other provisions, the act exempts multistate ownership of wholesale electric power facilities from federal securities regulation under the Public Utility Holding Company Act of 1935. The act also gives FERC authority to order access to the electric transmission grid.

National Environmental Policy Act (NEPA) An environmental law signed in 1970 by U.S. President Richard Nixon. The law establishes a national policy that requires federal agencies and the programs they fund to consider the environmental impacts of that action prior to taking any "major" or "significant" action.

Natural gas A mixture of hydrocarbon compounds and small amounts of various nonhydrocarbons (such as carbon dioxide, helium, hydrogen sulfide, and nitrogen, for example) existing in the gaseous phase or in solution with crude oil in natural underground reservoirs.

Natural gas hydrates Icelike mixtures of methane and water, sometimes found in permafrost or in sediments beneath the ocean floor.

Natural gas liquids (NGL) Portions of natural gas that are liquefied at the surface in lease separators, field facilities, or gas processing plants, leaving dry natural gas. They include, but are not limited to, ethane, propane, butane, natural gasoline, and condensate.

Nonattainment areas Regions of the country that do not meet the National Ambient Air Quality Standards of the Clean Air Act for one or more of the seven regulated air pollutants.

Octane number A rating used to grade the relative antiknock properties of various gasolines. A high-octane fuel has better antiknock properties than one with a low number.

Offset policy Policy that new industrial plants could not be built in nonattainment areas as defined by the Clean Air Act, unless pollution from existing factories was reduced enough to compensate for the pollution expected from the new plant. A company wanting to build in a nonattainment area must keep its own emissions down in that area or buy emissions offsets from other companies.

Offshore platform A fixed structure from which wells are drilled offshore for the production of oil and natural gas.

Oil shale A fine-grained, sedimentary rock that contains the solid substance *kerogen*, which is partially formed oil. Kerogen can be extracted in the form of shale oil by heating the shale.

OPEC The Organization of Petroleum Exporting Countries is an international organization of twelve oil-exporting developing nations that coordinates and unifies the petroleum policies of its member countries. It was founded at a meeting in 1960 in Baghdad, Iraq, by Iran, Iraq, Kuwait, Saudi Arabia, and Venezuela. They were later joined by Algeria, Angola, Indonesia, Libya, Nigeria, Qatar, and the United Arab Emirates.

Outer Continental Shelf (OCS) A gently sloping underwater plain that extends seaward from the coast. Technically, it includes only those lands between the end of state jurisdiction (three miles in most areas, but about ten miles for Texas and parts of Florida) and the two-hundred-meter water depth. However, the term *OCS* is now used by the government and the petroleum industry to include both the continental shelf and the continental slope to the twenty-five-hundred-meter water depth.

Overthrust belt A geological system of faults and basins in which geologic forces have thrust layers of older rock above strata of newer rock that might contain oil or natural gas. The Eastern Overthrust Belt runs from eastern Canada through Appalachia into Alabama. The Western Overthrust Belt runs from Alaska through western Canada and the Rocky Mountains into Central America.

Particulates Tiny particles of soot, ash, and other solids or liquids that are emitted into the air.

Passive solar Architectural designs in buildings that take advantage of site and building materials to enhance the amount of solar radiation that can be turned into useful interior heat during cold periods and that minimize absorption of solar heat during warm periods.

Permeability A measure of the capacity of a rock or stratum to allow water or other fluids like oil to pass through it. See *porosity*.

Petrochemicals Chemicals derived from crude oil or natural gas, include ammonia, carbon black, and thousands of various organic chemicals.

Petroleum Strictly speaking, crude oil. In a broader sense, it refers to all hydrocarbons, including oil, natural gas, natural gas liquids, and related products.

Photovoltaic The conversion of sunlight directly into electricity by means of solar cells.

Plutonium A radioactive element that can be a raw material in the manufacture of nuclear weapons or a waste product of processes yielding atomic energy.

Porosity A measure of the amount of void space or pores within rock that affects the amount of liquids and gases (such as crude oil and natural gas) that rock can contain.

Powerplant and Industrial Fuel Use Act (FUA) This law, passed in the United States in 1978, prohibited utilities and large industrial consumers from using natural gas as a boiler fuel in new installations. Falling natural gas demand and prices finally spurred the repeal in 1987 of sections of the FUA that restricted the use of natural gas by industrial users and electric utilities. As a result of the repeal, natural gas and oil could again be used to fuel large new baseload electric power plants, and restrictions on gas and oil-burning industrial boilers, turbines, and engines were lifted. FUA restrictions continued that had allowed industrial cogenerators to use natural gas if they met certain operating conditions. Restrictions were eliminated for all new facilities constructed after 1987.

Prevention of Significant Deterioration (PSD) areas Areas that meet or exceed Clean Air Act standards for specific pollutants. Emissions in these areas are regulated so that the air quality does not deteriorate beyond certain levels.

Price control Setting limits on prices (usually maximum limits) by government order.

Primary recovery Extracting oil from a well by allowing only the natural water or gas pressure in the reservoir to force the petroleum to come to the surface, without pumping or other assistance. Also called *flush production.*

Production A term commonly used for natural resources actually taken out of the ground.

Proved reserves An estimate of the amount of oil or natural gas believed to be recoverable from known reservoirs under existing economic and operating conditions.

Public lands Any land or land interest owned by the federal government within the fifty states. The term does not include offshore federal lands or lands held in trust for Native American groups.

Public Utility Holding Company Act (PUHCA) Legislation enacted in 1935 to protect utility stockholders and consumers from financial and economic abuses of utility holding companies. Unless utilities have structured their operations to avoid PUHCA, the company is subject to extensive regulation by the Securities and Exchange Commission (SEC). Amended by the National Energy Policy Act of 1992 so that multistate power generation subsidiaries would exempt a party from PUHCA.

Pyrolysis Application of heat to pulverized coal in the absence of air to break the coal molecules into liquids and gases.

R & D Research and development.

Reclamation Restoring land to its original condition by regrading contours and replanting after the land has been mined, drilled, or otherwise undergone alteration from its original state.

Recoverable resources An estimate of resources, including oil and/or natural gas, both proved and undiscovered, that would be economically extractable under specified price-cost relationships and certain technological conditions.

Rem A measure of radiation exposure, specifically the dosage of radiation that will cause the same amount of biological injury to human tissue as one roentgen of X-ray or gamma ray dosage. Usually used in fractional amounts, such as millirems (1 millirem equals 0.001 rem).

Rental The amount periodically paid by a leaseholder to a landowner for the right to use property for purposes set out in the lease.

Reserves Proportion of the energy (natural gas, for example) resource commercially recoverable under current economic conditions with current technology. Reserves are those resources believed to be recoverable with the highest degree of confidence.

Reserves-to-Production or R/P ratio Ratio of remaining recoverable reserves to the current rate of production.

Reservoir Geological formation holding an accumulation of oil and/or natural gas.

Residual fuel Heavy oil used by utilities and industries for fuel.

Retort Any closed vessel or facility for heating a material to cause a chemical reaction.

Retorting Any of a variety of methods by which a carbonaceous material is heated, generally above 700 degrees Fahrenheit, to decompose the material into gases, oils, tars, and carbon. Heat for retorting is obtained by burning a portion of the raw feed and/or fuels derived from the process. Oil shale is processed by retorting.

Retrofitting See *backfitting*.

Return on investment (rate of return) A measure of the profitability of a business enterprise. The general form is profit divided by investment, but the calculations can take many alternative forms. Investment can refer to stockholders' equity only or also can include long-term borrowed funds for all resources available to a company that are total assets. Profits can be measured before or after corporate income taxes.

Royalty A payment to a landowner or mineral rights owner (which can be a government body or private party) by a leaseholder on each unit of resource produced. Oil and natural gas royalties are paid in cash, as a percentage of the value of production. However, in some cases, the landowner or mineral rights owner receives a percentage of the actual petroleum produced.

Sarbanes-Oxley Act of 2002 Also known as the Public Company Accounting Reform and Investor Protection Act of 2002 and commonly called SOX. This federal law was enacted in the United States in 2002 in response to a number of major corporate and accounting scandals, including those affecting the former energy giant Enron that resulted in a decline of public trust in accounting and reporting practices. The bill is named for sponsors Senator Paul

Sarbanes (D-Maryland) and Representative Michael G. Oxley (R-Ohio). The legislation is wide ranging and establishes new or enhanced standards for all U.S. public company boards, management, and public accounting firms.

SASOL South African Synthetic Oil Limited. A government-owned synthetic fuel facility located in Secunda, South Africa, where South African coal is gasified and a broad range of synthetic fuels are produced.

Scrubber A pollution control device inside the stack of a coal-burning facility that uses liquid spray to remove pollutants, especially sulfur dioxide, from emissions. The process itself is called *flue gas desulphurization.*

Sedimentary rock Rock formed of sediments, usually deposited in a marine environment, such as shale or sandstone. Petroleum is found in sedimentary rock.

Seismic exploration A method of prospecting for oil or gas by sending shock waves into the earth. Reflections of the shock waves that bounce off rock strata are recorded on magnetic tape. The time it takes for the wave to return to the surface can be interpreted by experts to indicate the depth of specific strata and the composition of intermediate strata.

Service well A well drilled in a known oil or natural gas field to inject liquids to enhance recovery, dispose of saltwater, or for purposes other than actual production.

Severance tax A tax paid to a state by producers of mineral resources (including oil and gas) in the state. The tax is usually levied as a percent of the value of the oil or gas severed from the earth. It also may be expressed as a specific amount per barrel of oil or thousand cubic feet of gas.

Shale oil The hydrocarbon substance produced from the decomposition of kerogen when oil shale is heated in an oxygen-free environment. Raw shale oil resembles a heavy, viscous, low-sulfur crude but can be upgraded to produce a good quality sweet crude.

Sludge In discussions of environmental controls, the mudlike residue that results from the cleaning process of scrubbers or certain other devices designed to prevent solid particulates from entering the environment.

Solar thermal energy The use of the sun's heat for space heating (or through refrigeration coils for cooling).

Solvent refined coal (SRC) A coal extract derived through the use of solvents. Crushed coal is mixed in a solvent at high temperature and pressure in the presence of hydrogen. The process produces a solid (SRC-I) or liquid (SRC-II) that is free of ash and sulfur. After processing, the ash is removed from the solvent and the solvent is recycled.

Sour gas Gas found in its natural state containing enough sulfur to make it impractical to use without purifying.

Sour crude oil Crude oil that contains significant amounts of hydrogen sulfide. Often less valuable than sweet crude oil.

Spent shale Shale that is left over after kerogen (shale oil) has been removed.

State OCS jurisdiction The area where coastal states own mineral rights on offshore lands. In general, the boundary is three nautical miles out from shore, except off Texas and the Gulf Coast of Florida, where the states own three leagues (about ten nautical miles) out from shore.

Steam coal A quality of coal used by utilities for generating steam to make electricity. Usually has a lower heat content than metallurgical coal.

Stocks inventories Widely used in the petroleum industry to designate inventories of crude oil and other oil products at refineries, bulk terminals, and in pipelines.

Strata Layers of rock.

Strategic Petroleum Reserve (SPR) A stockpile of oil maintained by the United States. The U.S. government purchases crude oil and pumps it into underground salt domes for use in case of an import supply interruption, shortage, or other emergency.

Stratigraphic test A well drilled specifically to obtain detailed information on the composition of a rock formation that might lead to the discovery of oil or natural gas.

Stripper gas well A well that produces an average of fewer than than sixty thousand cubic feet a day, measured over a ninety-day period. The nation's natural gas stripper wells produce approximately 1.5 trillion cubic feet of gas per year (about 8 percent of U.S. production).

Stripper oil well A well capable of producing no more than ten barrels of oil a day. Some 80 percent of U.S. oil wells are now classified as marginal wells. These wells produce 860,000 barrels of oil per day (nearly 20 percent of U.S. production).

Subbituminous coal Coal ranked between bituminous and lignite in heat value and overall quality. It has a range of heat values between 16.5 and 23 million Btu per ton.

Sulfur dioxide emissions Heavy, pungent, toxic gases released when fuel containing sulfur is burned.

Sweet crude oil Crude oil that is low in sulfur. Often more valuable than sour crude oil.

Synthetic crude oil (syncrude) A crude oil derived from processing a carbonaceous material. Oil extracted from shale or unrefined oil from coal conversion plants are syncrudes.

Synthetic fuels (synfuels) Fuels that are produced through complex chemical conversions of such natural fossil substances as coal and oil shale. Synthetic fuels are comparable in chemical structure and energy value to oil products and natural gas.

Synthetic gas Gas made from solid hydrocarbons such as coal, oil shale, or tar sands.

Tanker Oceangoing ship specially designed for carrying crude oil and other liquid petroleum products.

Tar sands Rocks containing highly viscous hydrocarbons (other than coal or oil shale) that are not recoverable by primary production methods. That is, the hydrocarbons in tar sands cannot readily move as a fluid under their own reservoir energy. The hydrocarbons in heavy oil sands, in contrast, will flow slowly under their own reservoir energy.

Tcf Trillion cubic feet. The cubic foot is a standard unit of measure for quantities of gas at atmospheric pressure.

Therm A measure of heat content. One therm equals one hundred thousand British thermal units.

Thermal recovery An enhanced recovery method using heat to thin oils that are too thick to flow to producing wells. One method uses the heat created by injecting oxygen and starting a fire in the well. Another consists of injecting steam.

Tight reservoirs Soil or rock formations with low permeability to oil, water, or natural gas.

Trans-Alaska Pipeline The eight-hundred-mile-long Trans Alaska Pipeline System (TAPS) is one of the largest pipeline systems in the world. It stretches from Prudhoe Bay on Alaska's North Slope through rugged terrain to Valdez, the northernmost ice-free port in North America. Since pipeline began in 1977, Alyeska Pipeline Service Company, the operator of TAPS, has transported over fifteen billion barrels of oil.

Undiscovered recoverable resources Resources outside of known fields, estimated from broad geologic knowledge and theory.

Unit train A train of at least one hundred cars specially designed to haul and unload coal.

Upstream The exploration and production portions of the oil and gas industry.

Viscosity The measure of a liquid's internal friction or of its resistance to flow.

Water quality standards Standards adopted by states under the Clean Water Act for quantities of pollution allowed in water bodies. Water quality standards are not the major method of pollution control under the Clean Water Act, which primarily designates required control technology rather than particular standards of water quality.

Waterflooding The most common enhanced recovery method (usually referred to as secondary recovery). Water is pumped into an oil reservoir to push the oil toward producing wells. This method of recovery is often used after a field's own internal pressure is no longer sufficient to provide adequate oil production.

Wetlands Lands with very moist soil, such as tidal flats or swamps.

Wildcatter An operator who drills the first well in an unproven territory.

Wilderness land Land withdrawn from development by Congress in order to preserve its pristine characteristics as set forth in the National Wilderness Preservation System Act of 1964.

Windfall Profits Tax A U.S. tax on crude oil production (actually an excise tax rather than a tax on profits). The tax is a specified percentage of the difference between the sales price in the field and a base price established by the government for each of various oil categories. The percentage and the base price both vary depending on how a given field had been treated under price control regulations. The base prices are automatically increased each year. Repeal of the tax was signed into law as part of the massive trade bill by President Ronald Reagan on August 24, 1988.

Withdrawal of government lands Restricting the use of government lands by holding them for specific public purposes. Such restrictions virtually always include prohibition of exploration for and production of oil, natural gas, or other minerals.

Bibliography

THE FOLLOWING BOOKS, publications, videos, and other documentary material were used either to compile information for this book or appeared to be excellent material for additional education about the petroleum industry.

The variety of the listings reflects the complexity of this industry. The listings below are a cross section of materials that include reference books, brochures, how-to books, and reflections of long-time industry career professionals. Check your local library or sites such as www.amazon.com for these and other books related to your area of interest.

Beck, Robert J. *Worldwide Petroleum Industry Outlook*, 20th ed. Tulsa, Okla.: PennWell Publishing, 2003.

Burleson, Clyde W. *Deep Challenge: Our Quest for Energy Beneath the Sea*. Burlington, Mass.: Gulf Professional Publishing, 2006.

Busby, Rebecca L., ed. *2006 International Petroleum Encyclopedia.* Tulsa, Okla.: PennWell Publishing, 2006.

Chandra, Vivek. *Fundamentals of Natural Gas: An International Perspective.* Tulsa, Okla.: PennWell Publishing, 2006.

Clark, James Anthony, and Michel T. Halbouty. *Spindletop: The True Story of the Oil Discovery That Changed the World.* Lanham, Md.: Taylor Trade Publishing, 2002.

Fundamentals of the Global Oil and Gas Industry. London: Petroleum Economist, 2006.

Johnston, David, and Daniel Johnston. *Introduction to Oil Company Financial Analysis.* Tulsa, Okla.: PennWell Publishing, 2005.

Kelly, Fred W. Jr. *Global Oil Finder: Autobiography of a Petroleum Geologist.* Bloomington, Ind.: Authorhouse, 2006.

Krasner, Sam. *The Oil Patch and Oil Man: From Depression to Inflation and Crisis.* Austin, Tex.: Sunbelt Eakin Press, 2004.

Miesner, Thomas O., and William L. Leffler. *Oil & Gas Pipelines in Nontechnical Language.* Tulsa, Okla.: PennWell Publishing, March 2006.

Montague, Kenneth E. Kenneth E. Montague Series in Oil and Business. (Author has written several books related to oil and business history.) College Station, Tex.: Texas A&M University Press.

Parra, Francisco. *Oil Politics: A Modern History of Petroleum.* London, England: I.B. Tauris, 2004.

Petroleum Extension Service. *A Dictionary for the Oil and Gas Industry.* Austin, Tex.: University of Texas, 2005.

Plunkett, Jack W. *Plunkett's Energy Industry Almanac 2007: Energy Industry Market Research, Statistics, Trends, and Leading Companies.* Houston, Tex.: Plunkett Research, Ltd., 2006.

Raymond, Martin S., and William L. Leffler. *Oil and Gas Production in Nontechnical Language*. Tulsa, Okla.: PennWell Publishing, 2005.

Roberts, Paul. *The End of Oil: On the Edge of a Perilous New World* (reprint ed.). New York: Mariner Books, 2005.

Shah, Sonia. *Crude: The Story of Oil*. New York: Seven Stories Press, 2006.

Society of Petroleum Engineers. *Profile: The Petroleum Industry* (video). Richardson, Tex.: Society of Petroleum Engineers.

So You Want to be a Roughneck? (video). Austin, Tex.: Petroleum Extension Service, The University of Texas at Austin.

U.S. Department of Labor. *Dictionary of Occupational Titles*. Washington, DC.

U.S. Department of Labor. *Occupational Outlook Handbook*, 2006–2007 ed. Washington DC: U.S. Department of Labor, Bureau of Labor Statistics, 2006.

Wheeler, Robert R. and Maurine Whited. *Oil: From Prospect to Pipeline*. Houston, Tex.: Gulf Publishing Co., 2005.

Yeomans, Matthew. *Oil: Anatomy of an Industry*. New York: New Press, 2004.

About the Author

Gretchen Dewailly Krueger is an award-winning energy communicator. As energy editor of *The Daily Advertiser* (Lafayette, Louisiana) in the 1980s, Krueger wrote, edited, and designed a weekly energy section, including a column that focused on key energy issues. While there, she won six awards for her coverage of the industry. She is a three-time winner of the Louisiana Mid-Continent Oil and Gas Association's top award. More recently, she won an award from the Texas Public Relations Association for her communications on a natural-gas pipeline project in southwestern Virginia.

The Bordelonville, Louisiana, native received a degree in English-Journalism from the University of Southwestern Louisiana in Lafayette (now the University of Louisiana-Lafayette).

She is currently Director of Communications for Spectra Energy, one of North America's leading midstream natural gas companies. Her husband, a semiretired veteran of the petroleum industry, continues to serve as her "in-house consultant." They live in the Houston, Texas, area.

$14.95
MAY 1 4 2008